Your First Home

A Buyer's Kit

For Condos and Houses!

Kimberley Marr, CAAP, ABR®

Self-Counsel Press
(a division of)
International Self-Counsel Press Ltd.
USA   Canada

Self-Counsel Press acknowledges the financial support of the Government of Canada through the Canada Book Fund (CBF) for our publishing activities.

Printed in Canada.

First edition: 2012

Library and Archives Canada Cataloguing in Publication

Marr, Kimberley

Your first home: a buyer's kit / Kimberley Marr.

ISBN 978-1-77040-095-5

1. House buying — Canada. 2. Real property — Purchasing — Canada. I. Title.

HD1379.E44 2011   643'.120971   C2011-904552-4

Amortization schedules starting on page 39 used with permission from The Mortgage Centre/ R.D.M. Financial Consultants.

MIX
Paper from
responsible sources
FSC
www.fsc.org   FSC® C004071

Self-Counsel Press
(a division of)
International Self-Counsel Press Ltd.

Bellingham, WA   North Vancouver, BC
USA   Canada

Contents

Notice to Readers

Laws are constantly changing. Every effort is made to keep this publication as current as possible. However, the author, the publisher, and the vendor of this book make no representations or warranties regarding the outcome or the use to which the information in this book is put and are not assuming any liability for any claims, losses, or damages arising out of the use of this book. The reader should not rely on the author or the publisher of this book for any professional advice. Please be sure that you have the most recent edition.

Note: The fees quoted in this book are correct at the date of publication. However, fees are subject to change without notice. For current fees, please check with the court registry or appropriate government office nearest you.

Prices, commissions, fees, and other costs mentioned in the text or shown in samples in this book probably do not reflect real costs where you live. Inflation and other factors, including geography, can cause the costs you might encounter to be much higher or even much lower than those we show. The dollar amounts shown are simply intended as representative examples.

Readers should consult with qualified professionals in the province or territory of purchase for specific, personalized service and advice.

REALTOR® — The trademarks REALTOR®, REALTORS®, and the REALTOR® logo are controlled by the Canadian Real Estate Association (CREA) and identify real estate professionals who are members of CREA. Used under license.

MLS® — The trademarks MLS®, Multiple Listing Service®, and the associated logos are owned by the Canadian Real Estate Association (CREA) and identify the quality of services provided by the real estate professionals who are members of CREA. Used under license.

Acknowledgements

A uthoring this book was a labour of love, but I didn't create this book alone; it was truly a team effort. I wish to acknowledge and thank the following people: Tom Hogg and Kevin Macklem, R.D.M. Financial Consultants Ltd., The Mortgage Centre; Kevin Haxell, Haxell Law; Lorne Barsky, RZCD Law; Jeffery L. Rolke, TD Waterhouse, Toronto-Dominion Bank; Gary Bostock, Pillar to Post Home Inspection; and Christine Mitchell, Broker/Manager, RE/MAX Professionals Inc. Brokerage. We meet again; it's amazing what one phone call can turn into. Linda Sansom, Broker/General Manager, RE/MAX Professionals Inc., Brokerage, I feel so at ease when I know you are there to "take care of things" — and you know all the rules! Thanks to each of you for spending the time reviewing the specific chapters in the book relating to your specialty and sharing your expertise. Your technical and professional advice is invaluable and will certainly help readers and first-time home buyers on their home-buying journey.

Special thanks to the Self-Counsel Press team, and Eileen Velthuis, Managing Editor — this book came to be in a roundabout way. I thank you for offering me this opportunity and for guiding me throughout the process. Tanya Lee Howe, Editor, your expertise in helping to pull the manuscript together, organizing it in such a way that is logical and helpful to the reader is an amazing talent.

To Mom and Dad — you are the best! You have always believed in me and encouraged me to follow my dreams. Thank you for being there through thick and thin.

My own life has been enriched by great family, friends, and mentors who have inspired and encouraged me immeasurably. I enjoy and cherish every minute we spend together. Your patience, love, and support have allowed me to grow and follow my passion. I look forward to spending more time in the future with all of you. Special thank-you to my family, as well as PA, DB, MB, ME, RE, D+DH, MJ, HF, BJ, KL, BV, TS, DS, and SS — you know who you are — thank you for believing in me. I am honoured and blessed to know you and have you in my life.

Finally, I would like to thank my clients and readers. Throughout my career I have had the good fortune of meeting and working with some of the finest people on the planet. I am honoured to have been a part of such an important and personal aspect of your lives. You are the reason I love what I do. This book is for you.

Introduction

Buying your first home is an exciting, big step. There is a need amongst first-home buyers for sound guidance, information, and disclosure of facts. Home ownership is a major decision; it is not just about acquiring shelter or making an investment. When you purchase a home you are buying a lifestyle. It is a place where dreams can become reality; for example:

- Enjoying the warmth of a fireplace in the family room.

- Preparing a home-cooked dinner in a spacious kitchen.

- Fulfilling a gardening hobby or inviting friends and family over for a barbecue.

Home is where we raise our children and share life experiences with family and friends. For many, home has even become a place of business thanks to the virtual office options we have today.

Your home may be the largest financial investment you will make. For many, real estate is the cornerstone of their net worth — often the equity in a home is the resource that enhances finances during retirement. Buying a home can be an emotionally charged, confusing, and potentially overwhelming experience.

If you simply mention that you are considering buying your first home, you are sure to get plenty of advice from well-meaning family and friends. While being well informed about the home-buying process and having experience is beneficial, often the advice and information is confusing or incomplete and may be based on someone else's house-buying experience and personal results. Each situation is different.

Now that you are thinking about this important financial decision, you will begin to notice information and advertisements about various aspects of the home-buying process. Walk into a bank and you will see brochures, posters, and booklets offering myriad mortgage products and options. Which mortgage product is best for you?

Driving around town, you may notice open house signs, or new home billboards, each offering something special and distinct. Open up the real estate section of the newspaper and you will find pages of advertisements offering different housing options and special financing programs.

Turn on the television or surf the Internet and you will hear different opinions about the market, the inventory, prices, interest rates, which areas are hot, and a host of other real estate related topics. You may be asking yourself:

- Where do I begin?

- Who should I contact?

- How much can I afford?

This can be overwhelming and somewhat scary. You may feel that you are on an information and option overload! At this stage, what you really need is an organized *plan*. Having knowledge helps to alleviate fear. Knowledge also provides you with the confidence to make prudent, well-thought-out decisions.

Plan ahead, gather information, and ask lots of questions. Time and effort needs to be spent on your part in determining your unique needs, objectives, and financial goals. An informed buyer is a successful buyer.

This book is the result of more than 23 years of real estate practice and experience. I have worked with lenders and mortgage brokers, home inspectors, insurance agents, real estate lawyers, accountants, new home builders, and contractors — all of whom have generously shared their time and expertise with me throughout my career. The process of purchasing real estate has several different moving parts and is a team effort. Often when we are embarking on a new project or journey, we don't even know what we don't know; this book will share the knowledge and experience that I have acquired as part of a team of professionals. A team of professionals in the real estate industry have reviewed the chapters related to their expertise and have added their insights and advice. First-time buyers need to have this information and understand the process and tasks to consider and complete before buying a home.

My goal in writing this book is to show you a systematic, objective-oriented home-buying process. This book will provide you with information and resources so that you can create your own Home Buyer Plan unique to your needs, wants, and wishes. It answers questions from people just like you, with similar concerns and desires. It offers straightforward answers and clear explanations to help you feel more comfortable and confident in your home-buying decisions.

After reading this book, you will be better prepared to make decisions as well as understand the role of ancillary professionals — other professionals who may become a part of your home-buying team. You will be shown how to qualify for and obtain a mortgage as well as become familiar with mortgage "lingo" such as conventional versus high-ratio mortgages, and the programs that Canada Mortgage and Housing Corporation (CMHC) or Genworth Financial Canada offer first-time buyers in Canada. Information is also included about how to set up and track your home budget, understand government programs and regulations such as the Five Percent Down Payment Home Buyer Program, First Time Home Buyers' tax credit (HBTC), land transfer tax rebates, and Home Buyers' Plan (HBP) in relation to your RRSP. My favourite topic is tips for paying off your mortgage quickly thereby building your equity and net worth.

Tools and information are provided to assist you with defining your home needs, wants, and wish list including geographic considerations and housing types and styles. Information regarding the differences between purchasing a newly built home versus a resale home is also reviewed.

This book includes topics about understanding the roles of the real estate agent (also called a broker), lawyer, and home inspector. By understanding the real estate agent's duties as well as agency relationships, you will be better prepared to research and find a real estate professional to assist you with the buying process if you so choose. Lawyers are an important part of the real estate process; you will find information on legal considerations, agreements of purchase and sale, closing costs, and working with a lawyer. Home inspections and insurance highlights are also reviewed.

The book has been set up in a format to enable you to utilize it as a guide. It will help you with planning and executing your own Home Buyer Plan. The chapters of the book are organized in the order in which you will most likely deal with topics and items during your home-buying process. This book can be used as part of your systematic, objective-oriented plan, so go ahead, feel free to write notes and highlight sections to put this book to use. Write down your plans, thoughts, and ideas. As you progress, you will be assembling a team of professionals who can provide you with additional information and tools to help move you through the home-buying process.

Having knowledge is powerful. Your dreams, lifestyle, and goals are waiting. This book will provide you with information and tools to assist with your home-buying goals so that you can realize an enjoyable and successful first home purchase.

Stop being confused, overwhelmed, and afraid. Let's get started on your journey!

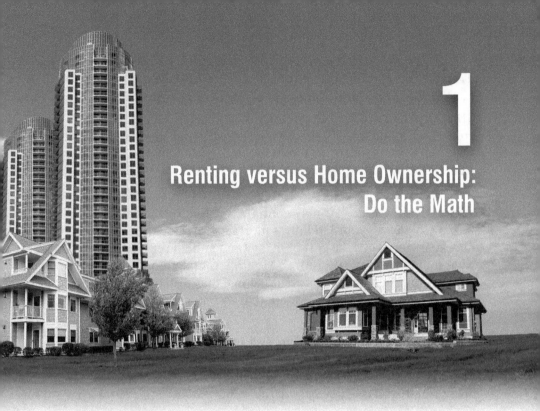

1

Renting versus Home Ownership: Do the Math

You may have heard that owning real estate is a good investment. You may also wonder if this is a good time to be investing in a home. Perhaps you've read that prices have been stable, and in some neighbourhoods, homes are increasing in value and have been for the past several years. Compared to the last three decades, interest rates are exceptionally low. Combined, these factors make home ownership attractive, but don't forget the lifestyle benefits of owning a home.

One of the lifestyle benefits is being able to put your own creative mark on your home. It is your own space to decorate as you wish. When you rent, you may not want to spend the time and money decorating (e.g., painting, adding nicer light fixtures, upgrading old carpeting or appliances). This is the psychological plus of home ownership!

Let's compare renting versus buying and owning a home. Everyone needs a place to live. Consider that when you are renting, you are probably paying a mortgage — your landlord's mortgage! Over time, you are paying off your landlord's mortgage, and for that, your landlord is grateful. But where does this leave you in the future? Have you ever calculated just how much money you are contributing toward your landlord's mortgage?

1. Renting Is Paying Someone Else's Mortgage

Let's assume you are renting for $1,500 per month, which equals $18,000 per year. Over five years (assuming the rent does not increase), this equals $90,000. Over ten years, this equals $180,000. Over 25 years (which is a popular mortgage amortization time frame), this would equate to $450,000!

What do you have to show for it? Probably a stack of rent receipts. Even worse, you may continue renting in the future, continuing to pay off your landlord's mortgage. Although your income may keep pace with the cost of living (and annual rental increases), what happens when you retire? Monthly rental amounts may continue to rise, but your retirement income may not, or worse, it may become less. This may necessitate that you move to a smaller home or farther away, or both.

Buying your first home is an exciting and emotionally charged event. It is also a major life decision. As with most new experiences, you don't know what you don't know. How can you ask questions about things you don't even know exist?

2. Build Your Own Equity

Why not channel your monthly shelter payment into your own mortgage and over time build equity and net worth for yourself? *Equity* is the difference between the home's value and what is owed on it. Over time, as you pay your mortgage, the principal loan balance decreases and, in some cases, the home's market value may increase.

Home ownership can be looked at as a forced savings account — especially if you commit to paying off a mortgage faster than the amortization period. It is possible that your mortgage can be paid off in 25 years (or sooner), and then you would own an asset — free and clear — that may even increase in value over time. Don't you think this would give you security and peace of mind?

Did you know that some mortgages offer a prepayment option that gives you the option to pay a little more each month or year toward the principal debt so that you can own your home even faster?

The low interest rates available at the time of this book's printing make the prospect of buying and owning your own home more possible. Home ownership can be a foundation for you to build security and wealth even if you earn ordinary income. In other words, you don't need to be wealthy to buy or own a home.

You may wonder if real estate values will continue to increase. Nobody has a crystal ball. Over the last 30 years, residential real estate has increased in most major markets, but who knows if this will continue and, if so, at what rate. Past performance is no guarantee of future results. Real estate is an investment, and like any other investment, there are pros and cons and risks.

Think about why you are considering home ownership. Try to look at real estate as a long-term investment — an investment that you get to live in and enjoy.

People also invest in stocks, mutual funds, and commodities. While these investments (although not the topic of this book) may or may not be good investments, and may or may not be part of your current or future financial plan, one thing we know is that you cannot *live* in a stock, mutual fund, or commodity, but you can live in your real estate investment.

Unlike most other investments, in Canada, currently there is no tax on your principal residence capital increase or gain. This means if your home increases in value by $100,000, when you sell, as a Canadian taxpayer, you are exempt from paying tax on the capital gain as long as it is your principal residence. Consult with a tax professional for additional information on the rules (especially if you were renting out a portion of or operating a business in the home while you lived in the home — special tax rules may apply).

Home ownership eliminates the possibility that you will be notified that an owner is selling the property and you may need to move in the future. Also, there is no more waiting around for the landlord or maintenance team to repair items. You are in control now!

3. Creating Your Home Buyer Plan

Uncertainty can make the home-buying process intimidating and scary, but it doesn't have to be that way. Fear, which is often linked to lack of knowing how to do something, can prevent you from taking action. You have taken a first big step by acquiring this book to educate yourself on how to accomplish your dream of buying your first home.

Some of the questions you should consider for your Home Buyer Plan include:

- Should you buy a brand new home or a resale home?

- Would you prefer a condo or a freehold ownership (and do you know the difference between the two)?

- What type of home appeals to you? Do you prefer a two-storey, bungalow, or split-level home? (Real estate professionals can provide insight into the types of homes that are popular and available in your price range.)

- Have you thought about what your budget is and how much you can afford?

- Should you speak with a bank manager or perhaps interview a mortgage broker, and what is the difference between the services and mortgage products they each provide?

- Where can you get the best mortgage interest rate, terms, and conditions?

- Do you need a real estate broker or sales representative? How can he or she assist you and does he or she represent you?

- Where can you find a real estate professional and what types of questions should you ask when you meet with him or her?

- Have you spoken with an accountant about potential tax benefits and obligations, and an insurance company or broker about insurance and liability options?

- Where do you think you would like to live?

- Do you plan to accelerate or prepay against the principal debt of your mortgage to pay off the home quicker? If so, what options do you require in your mortgage for this to be possible? What is the maximum annual prepayment contribution allowed and are there any fees or penalties?

- What mortgage amortization and term do you need and how does this tie in with your anticipated time frame for living in your first home?

There is no need to feel overwhelmed. It is understandable that you may not know where to begin and what to ask. As you read through this book, you will find the answers to things you were thinking about as well as information on other options and considerations you may not have thought about yet.

Many people spend more money on a home than any other single investment. There are also many lifestyle factors and decisions that you will take into consideration as you prepare your Home Buyer Plan. For example, how long do you anticipate you will live in your first home? Based on my experience, average first-time buyers live in their first home for approximately five years.

Other questions you will need to consider:

- How much space will you need during this time?

- Do you have the option of working from home, thereby needing adequate work space, and perhaps parking? If you work from home, a portion of your expenses may be tax deductible (check with your accountant to determine whether you qualify for this benefit and whether there are tax obligations and liability issues for conducting business in your home).

You will be paying a *shelter payment* to live somewhere. Consider directing what would otherwise be rental dollars (paying your landlord's mortgage) to your own mortgage, and work toward paying off the mortgage quickly — while at the same time building equity for yourself.

Timing is a factor in your decision to buy (i.e., should you rent for another year or two and save more money for your down payment)? Obviously you are the only one who can make this decision; however, in some cities prices continue to increase so by the time you save more money, the market may have changed. Additionally, the money you will have paid in rent could have been channelled into your mortgage, steadily paying off your mortgage debt and building equity during that time.

Once you have answered some of the questions we've just covered, you will find that your Home Buyer Plan is forming, and you will be able to focus on your next steps to buying a home.

I understand that you have never done this before, so the home-buying process is unfamiliar and perhaps overwhelming. Don't let fear prevent you from realizing your dream of owning your first home. You need information, guidance, and a Home Buyer Plan. If planned well, your single largest investment could well be your best investment.

So take a deep breath, focus, get organized, and proceed with confidence. Let's continue your Home Buyer Plan by reviewing mortgage qualifying and mortgage terms and conditions in Chapter 2.

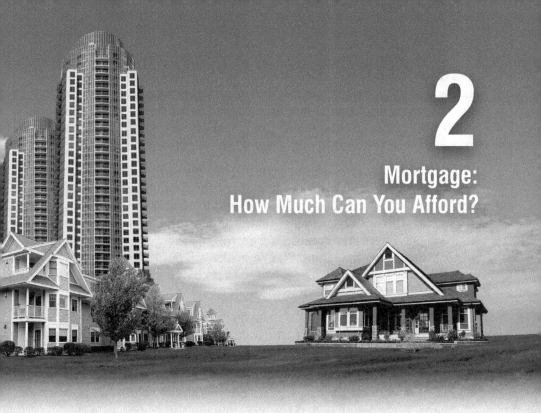

2

Mortgage: How Much Can You Afford?

A logical starting point when buying a home is to determine how much money you have to spend. Most first-time buyers don't have enough money to pay cash for their home so they need a mortgage.

A *mortgage* is a lien or charge recorded against the home in favour of the lender. It is an agreement or contract between a *borrower* (i.e., home buyer) who wants to borrow money in order to purchase a home and a *lender* (i.e., lending institution or person) willing to loan the money. The mortgage contains terms that the borrower agrees to with the lender. In return for the loan, the lender wants something to assure that the borrower will pay back the money — this is called *collateral*, which is normally the home that is purchased.

The lender also wants a *promise* that the borrower will pay back the money. The lender evaluates the risk in lending the money. Although the lender has the home as collateral, it really doesn't want your home (it's not in the business of collecting property that is in default of the owner's mortgage payment). Lenders want you to repay the borrowed money with interest. Lenders, more specifically financial institutions, make a profit by borrowing money from their customers through deposits, such as Guaranteed Investment Certificates (GICs), and other interest-bearing products at one rate then turning around and lending this money to borrowers at a higher rate. The profit is the difference between the interest rate paid by the lender to use the funds on deposit and the interest rate it charges the borrower (the "spread"), less the costs to originate and service the mortgage.

The lender underwrites the loan by starting with a credit check on the borrower. This gives the lender insight about borrowing and repayment track records and how the borrower uses credit. It tells the lender whether a borrower regularly and historically pays bills on time. This is important because if a borrower has a poor repayment history, the lender may think that he or she will not repay the mortgage loan on time, so the lender may either charge a higher interest rate to offset the risk or decline the loan.

If your credit report confirms that you have a good repayment history, the lender will classify you as good or an "A" customer and will want to see proof that you have a job. The lender will request a letter from your employer outlining your salary and stating how long you have been employed there.

If you are self-employed, this makes things a little trickier. In this case, depending on the lender, you will be requested to provide the past two or three years' worth of notices of assessment, and possibly tax returns and/or financial statements.

1. Understanding Mortgage Products

Mortgages are products, and they contain different options, terms, and conditions. The type of mortgage product you choose will depend on your individual short- and long-term financial goals and plans. It is difficult to be aware of all the different types of mortgage products on the market (keep in mind that the banks and lenders are always trying to impress upon you why their mortgage products are the best). There is more to a mortgage product than just comparing the interest rate and the term. Let's start with a general overview of the types of mortgage products that are available.

1.1 Conventional mortgage

A conventional mortgage is a mortgage loan that is equal to or less than 80 percent of the lending value of the property (i.e., the purchase price or market value, whichever is less). In other words, the down payment is at least 20 percent of the purchase price or market value. Most buyers use savings or a combination of investments and savings to make up the down payment. However, there may be other options to source or arrange for a portion of the down payment (more on this in Chapter 4).

1.2 High-ratio mortgage

If your down payment is less than 20 percent of the lending value or purchase price, whichever is less, your mortgage will be considered a high-ratio mortgage, which usually requires mortgage loan insurance. The insurance insures the lender against default. You, the borrower, pay for this insurance; your lender usually adds the mortgage loan insurance premium to your mortgage, or it can request that you pay it in full on closing. Note that applicable provincial sales tax is charged to the default insurance premium; however, the sales tax will not be added to the mortgage amount — it is payable on closing as part of your closing costs.

There are a couple of insurers that provide mortgage loan insurance: Canada Mortgage and Housing Corporation (CMHC) and Genworth Financial Canada.

1.3 Second mortgage

The second mortgage sits behind the first mortgage; the home is normally used as collateral. This means that if the home is sold, the proceeds of the sale pay off the "first" mortgage first, and the balance pays the "second" mortgage. As a point of interest, property taxes and condominium fees rank ahead of the first mortgage and upon sale are paid out first *before* the mortgage or any other junior liens.

Typically a second mortgage carries a higher interest rate and is for a shorter time frame than the first mortgage. Occasionally, secondary financing is used to assist a home buyer with coming up with a portion of the down payment. You will still be required to qualify to carry the two mortgages; however, utilizing a first and second mortgage may be advantageous when a buyer is very close to reaching a conventional financing down payment. Doing this will offset the mortgage insurance premium. This is something to discuss with your lender if you find yourself very close to meeting the 20 percent down payment required for conventional financing. A comparison of the interest rate cost, combined with any other legal and registration expenses versus the cost of mortgage default insurance will determine if this strategy is worthwhile.

1.4 Vendor Take Back (VTB)

Occasionally, a seller is willing to hold a portion of or possibly the entire mortgage. In this case, on closing, the seller secures the mortgage amount (the debt) on the property similar to what a bank or financial institution does (i.e., the home is used as collateral). The interest rate and terms of this type of mortgage are negotiated between the seller and the buyer. This type of mortgage is less common than traditional bank financing; however, in some cases the seller may offer or be willing to hold a mortgage. Some sellers who do not need the equity in their real estate (especially if they have no mortgage) consider this an investment.

1.5 Builder's mortgage

Occasionally, new home builders offer financing assistance as an incentive (and convenience) for buyers to purchase one of their new homes or condominiums. Builders may have an arrangement with a lender to *buy down* the prevailing interest rate or offer to lock in the interest rate until the home is built and you close (which could be several months to a few years in the future). For instance, assuming the current market interest rate is 5 percent, and the builder offers you a 3.5 or 2.9 percent rate, the builder would be paying the difference between the current rate and whatever rate is offered for the period of the term — this is what is meant by "buying down" the rate.

While this may be an attractive and more affordable way to enter into home ownership, read the fine print and get legal advice. Some builders may add this extra amount they paid to buy down the rate to the sale price of the home. Often the term of the mortgage the builder offers is short (e.g., one or two years), after which the mortgage loan becomes due and payable and you will need to arrange your own mortgage elsewhere at current rates. If interest rates have increased, this could create an affordability or qualifying problem for you. Determine if you will qualify for the mortgage at an anticipated higher rate. Consider worst-case scenarios with interest rates and how they may affect you in the future. Understand in advance what your responsibilities will be, and ensure that you get appropriate legal advice before you agree to this type of mortgage.

1.6 Closed mortgage

With a closed mortgage, you are "locked in" for a specific amount of time (e.g., three, five, seven, or ten years). This is known as your *term*.

You commit to the lender for a pre-defined period of time. It has the benefit of allowing you to feel comfortable knowing that your mortgage interest rate will not change during the locked-in term — meaning your monthly mortgage payments will stay the same during this time period. This helps for budgeting and cash-flow purposes.

However, with a closed mortgage, unless you have a prepayment privilege included with your mortgage agreement, you may not have the option to prepay more than the predetermined amount of the principal balance before the expiration of the term without paying a penalty. If you decide to sell your home prior to the expiry of the term, this may cost you a considerable amount of money in penalties. It is imperative that you find out, negotiate, and understand your prepayment and discharge options in advance with the lender to minimize costly penalties in the future.

Normally, a lower interest rate is associated with a closed mortgage, and it is possible to obtain prepayment privileges and early discharge terms (often limited to three months' interest penalty) with a closed mortgage. Make sure that you understand in advance what your terms and conditions will be with a closed mortgage. It is very important to know if a prepayment penalty exists (it usually does) and the amount the penalty will be before you agree to the mortgage; otherwise, this could be a very costly surprise. Ask and get the answer in writing! Consult with your lawyer prior to committing to any mortgage.

1.7 Open mortgage

Generally, an open mortgage is the opposite of a closed mortgage in that it has no prepayment penalty and is normally more flexible. Usually open mortgages are for shorter terms (e.g., six months, one or two years), and they usually come with higher interest rates because the lender is aware that you may pay back the loan early. Many lenders let you convert an open mortgage to a closed mortgage at some point in the future, although you may have to pay a fee to do so.

1.8 Fixed rate mortgage

A fixed rate mortgage has a preset interest rate that remains the same for the entire term. You have the comfort of knowing that each month you will make the same mortgage payment. Usually the amount of your payment goes toward both reducing the outstanding principal debt as well as interest and is decided at the outset of the mortgage. Over time, the allocation of what is attributed towards principal (versus interest) changes as more goes towards principal reduction. Keep in mind that most mortgages are front-loaded with interest at the beginning. (More about this and how to pay off a mortgage sooner in Chapter 3).

1.9 Variable or adjustable rate mortgage

The variable or adjustable rate mortgage is a little trickier. The Bank of Canada sets its *overnight* rate (i.e., the rate it lends to the banks) and the banks then add their *spread* and that ends up as the *prime rate*. When the Bank of Canada increases or decreases the rate that it lends, the banks usually follow suit with their prime rate, which in turn impacts variable rate mortgages. It is important to understand that not all banks or lenders use the term "prime rate" for their mortgages; some use terms such as "base rate" or "mortgage prime rate" which could have different definitions. Check the standard charge terms for the lender to determine if they actually use the terms the way you expect. Depending on the terms of the mortgage, this could affect you in a couple of ways:

1. The monthly amount you pay could change when the interest rate changes, making it more difficult to budget your monthly cash flow should rates increase.

2. The monthly mortgage amount remains fixed (does not change), but the percentage attributed towards interest and principal repayment changes. For example, if the interest rate increases, this reduces the amount you pay off each month toward the outstanding principal debt as more of your payment is applied to interest and less towards principal. What this also means is that your amortization period changes — it goes up, meaning it will take you longer to pay off the mortgage. However, if interest rates fall, this has a positive effect as the amount attributed to principal reduction is increased and the amortization period is shortened.

The major difference between fixed and variable or adjustable rate mortgages is the risk factor. You will need to consider whether or not you are more comfortable with a fixed monthly or biweekly payment. Or, whether or not you should take the risk of a variable or adjustable rate that may save you money, but may also cost you more money if rates rise. Normally, the interest rate for a variable rate mortgage is slightly lower.

Consideration needs to be given to where interest rates are at the time of this book's printing because they are at affordable, low levels. Will interest rates drop much in the future? Who knows what will occur with rates. Conservative buyers often choose a fixed rate mortgage at these low-rate levels because they want the security and comfort of knowing that their monthly or biweekly mortgage payments will be the same over the term of their mortgage.

If you choose a variable rate mortgage, consider being qualified or approved for the higher fixed rate, just in case rates increase because you don't want to be "house poor." In other words, you don't want to be in a situation where you are short of cash for discretionary items or have trouble meeting other financial obligations such as vehicle payments or credit card bills due to the fact that too large a portion of your income is being spent on home-related expenses (mortgage, property taxes, maintenance, and utilities).

Some lenders make it mandatory that you qualify for a higher fixed rate term. Be careful and budget conservatively in anticipation of a potential interest rate increase. Speak with a mortgage professional for the details and qualifying rules related to your situation.

1.10 Convertible mortgage

A convertible mortgage is a variable-rate or short-term (e.g., 6 to 12 months) fixed-rate mortgage that can be converted to a longer term fixed-rate mortgage (e.g., three, five, seven, or ten years) at any time during the term. If you would like to take advantage of lower rates on short-term or variable mortgages but feel that interest rates may rise, the convertible mortgage offers you the ability of being able to convert to a longer term fixed-rate mortgage. Usually these are closed mortgages as opposed to open mortgages. Again, be mindful of the difference in the mortgage payment when you convert, and budget accordingly.

Plan ahead and be prepared. Speak with your mortgage professional and ideally your lawyer to understand the terms, conditions, restrictions, and options you may have with your mortgage.

2. Getting Pre-Approved for a Mortgage

How much you can afford based on lender underwriting criteria, and how much you feel comfortable spending can be two different numbers. A good starting point is to find out what you are *qualified* to borrow based on lender underwriting ratios. This normally begins with completing a mortgage application with a bank, a lender, or through a mortgage broker.

2.1 Obtain your credit report

Before you apply for a loan, it is a good idea to obtain a copy of your credit report and check it to make sure that it is accurate. There are two main credit reporting agencies: Equifax Canada Inc. (www.equifax.ca), and TransUnion of Canada Inc. (www.transunion.ca). Contact either company to obtain your credit report.

You establish a credit file when you borrow money and pay it back. Your credit file details how you use credit and when you make payments. The information in your file is based on information given to the credit bureaus by creditors such as credit card companies and banks. Your credit report will show your payment history.

On your credit report you will notice an R or I preceding a number (e.g., R1, R2, I1, I2). The R indicates *revolving* credit such as a credit card, and an I means *installment* credit such as a vehicle loan or student loan. The number indicates the time you take to pay the minimum amount due. For example, R1 or I1 means that you have made at least the minimum payment (or more) when it was due. R3 or I3 means you are 60 days behind the due date. A higher number is not good because it means you have been even later with your payment obligations.

Your credit report will also give you a credit score, known as the "Beacon Score" if it was obtained from Equifax; or "TransRisk Score" if obtained from TransUnion (e.g., 580, 630, 800). For simplicity, we will refer to it as your "credit score."

In the case of the credit score, the higher the number the better. Lenders and insurers have minimum credit score numbers in relation to down payment requirements and debt ratios. Having and maintaining good credit is important. Items that are used to calculate your credit score include your payment history (i.e., whether or not you make your payments on time), length of credit history, amounts you currently owe relative to your credit limits, number and frequency of new credit inquiries, as well as the type of credit loans you have (e.g., vehicle loans, credit card balances, lines of credit).

The lender will look at your credit report and credit score to determine the risk. If you have a credit score lower than 600, this will affect your ability to acquire a high-ratio mortgage with less than a 20 percent down payment. If your down payment is from non-traditional sources (e.g., a gift from family), the mortgage insurer may require a credit score of 650 for a high-ratio borrower with a loan value greater than 80 percent. Many variables are considered; the lender will look at the strength of the deal, especially if there is a co-borrower with a good credit score. Visit CMHC (www.cmhc-schl.gc.ca) for an outline of the criteria along with recommended credit scores for a variety of situations.

If you are obtaining a mortgage with other borrowers, the lender will look at each person's credit score. If one of the borrowers has a low score, it may affect the terms of the loan.

Occasionally, there are errors in your credit report. Mistakes could include credit history that isn't yours or inaccurate reporting of bill payment. Any inaccurate information or error may be used to calculate your credit score, which could be a problem for you. If you find any errors, you will need to contact the credit bureaus in writing. If you have any documents that can prove or support your situation, send the credit bureaus a copy with a written explanation. This could take a few months to investigate and resolve. Credit bureaus will correct false information only. If a situation occurred where you missed a payment due to a circumstance, you can ask that a comment be included on your credit file explaining the situation (e.g., credit fraud or identity theft). This may (or may not) be taken into consideration on your credit score. Your bank representative or mortgage broker may be able to provide guidance or assistance with respect to contacting the credit bureaus and remedying any errors efficiently.

Be careful when shopping for a mortgage not to trigger multiple credit checks, as your credit score on your credit report may be adversely affected by the number of credit check requests occurring — especially over a short time span. It could be interpreted as you opening many accounts due to financial difficulties and taking on too much debt. When working with a mortgage broker that shops the mortgage market on your behalf, request that only one credit check is performed and that this same credit report is used for all the lenders.

If you have no credit history, it is important to establish one because the lender will have no information to assess the risk. Consider obtaining a credit card, but make sure that you make timely payments. You will need to do this several months prior to applying for a mortgage to ensure that a period of time has passed in order to create a credit history.

If you need to repair and improve your credit history, it will take some time. Your credit score is weighted towards your most recent performance; however, historical information, positive and negative, stays on the file for many years — the number of years varies depending on the item (e.g., bankruptcy, judgment) and the province or territory. Set up methods to ensure that your bills are paid on time; timely payments will improve your credit score. Consider automatic payment plans. Try to keep balances low on credit cards. If you can afford it, double up on your minimum required payments. Speak with your mortgage professional about the possibility of combining all your debts into one loan with a lower interest rate. Investigate different solutions. It is also important if you have student loans to be cognizant of your payment dates and obligations. Your credit score is an important element to obtaining a mortgage.

2.2 Understanding the difference between pre-qualify and pre-approval

Many buyers use the terms mortgage *pre-qualify* and mortgage *pre-approval* interchangeably. Many people believe they mean the same thing but this is not the case.

To be pre-qualified, you simply get an estimate of how much of a mortgage you will likely be able to qualify for based on current interest rates — a credit check and verification of employment have not been completed. During a pre-qualification meeting you present to the lender details of your income, expenses, assets, and liabilities to determine how much of a mortgage for which you will likely qualify.

A pre-approved mortgage is a formal application process. During the process you will be asked for information regarding your finances and creditworthiness — a credit check will be completed and your income will be verified. The lender or mortgage professional will use several factors, such as your income amount, credit score, employment records, and the amount of down payment you have, as guidelines to determine how much of a mortgage it will pre-approve for you. The lender will request a list of items including, but not limited to the following:

- A list of all your assets (e.g., vehicles, savings accounts, stocks, RRSPs, and GICs) along with an estimate of each asset's value.

- A list of all your liabilities (e.g., vehicle loans, credit cards, student loans) along with the balance owed for each.

- A letter from your employer confirming your employment including your income, position, and number of years with the company. Sometimes the lender may also request copies of T4 slips for the past couple of years. If you are self-employed you will need to provide notices of assessment and possibly tax returns and/or financial statements for the last two or three years, depending on the lender.

- Source of down payment funds. The lender will want to verify where the funds are coming from. If the down payment is being provided by family members, the lender may ask for a letter confirming the funds are a "gift" and do not need to be paid back.

- Personal information (i.e., social insurance number, as well as a source of photo identification such as a driver's licence or passport).

Remember, if you are applying for a pre-approved mortgage with a spouse, family member, or friend, all parties will be required to provide the above information.

Assuming everything checks out, you should be given a written mortgage pre-approval outlining the amount that the lender will commit to over a specific time frame and at what interest rate. The mortgage pre-approval may also specify certain conditions, so make sure that you understand the terms and conditions of the pre-approval. Special conditions and requirements may include that you pay off a credit card or debt.

The guaranteed lock-in time frame is an important date to keep in mind when searching for a home. This is a cut-off date or time frame for which your interest rate is guaranteed. Beyond that time frame, if interest rates have increased, you may find that it could affect what you are approved to spend and the cost could be higher. The guaranteed lock-in time frame is usually three or four months depending on the lender. Most of the time, buyers have no problem finding and closing on a home within this time frame. (If you are considering purchasing a new home that is not yet built with a longer anticipated closing date, check with the builder and your lender because often there are mortgage products or programs designed for new construction purchases.)

If interest rates decline, you should get the benefit of the lower rate. Check with the lender or mortgage professional about this, and where possible, get this in writing.

Having the interest rate locked in is one of the advantages of getting a pre-approved mortgage (versus a pre-qualified mortgage). Another benefit is that a pre-approved mortgage gives you leverage during the negotiations of your home purchase, which could turn out to be a competitive advantage in a hot real estate market.

With a pre-approved mortgage, some buyers consider making an offer to purchase a home without a finance condition; keep in mind that your lender will still want to have the property appraised to ensure you are paying a fair price. Additionally, if you are borrowing greater than 80 percent of the appraised value of the property, your lender will want CMHC or Genworth Financial Canada (or another high-ratio insurance company) to approve the transaction.

If the appraisal is for less than the purchase price, this could become a problem, and you may not be approved. Many buyers opt to include a short-term (i.e., one or two business days) finance condition to ensure that the appropriate property appraisals and insurance confirmations are obtained. This is a conservative and prudent strategy to ensure that everything is approved.

Speak with your mortgage professional about specific requirements. Don't assume just because you have a pre-approved mortgage that the property is approved for the mortgage. You want to be certain that you obtain written approval from the lender that your mortgage loan is approved before you waive or remove your finance condition.

2.3 Determine how much you can spend on a home

Lenders generally use two basic guidelines to determine how much they will lend you: Gross Debt Service Ratio (GDS) and Total Debt Service Ratio (TDS).

The Gross Debt Service Ratio (GDS) is where 32 percent (according to www.cmhc.ca, accessed October, 2011) of your gross income is used to determine what you qualify to pay for mortgage principal, interest, property tax, and heating per month (check with your lender or mortgage broker to confirm what you should use for the heating cost). In the case of condominium properties (e.g., apartment, townhouse, or other), you need also to factor 50 percent of the monthly mainte-nance fee into your calculation.

Figure out what 32 percent of your income is. For example, 32 percent of an an-nual income of $50,000 equals $16,000. Divide $16,000 by 12 which equals $1,333 per month.

a) Annual income $_____ x 0.32 = $ _____ divided by 12 = $_____ (principal; interest; tax; and heating per month; plus 50 percent of monthly condo fee, if applicable)

The Total Debt Service Ratio (TDS) is where 40 percent of your income is used to determine what you qualify to pay for above housing-related expenses plus all other loans (e.g., vehicle loans and credit cards). For example, an annual income of $50,000 x 0.40 equals $20,000. Divide $20,000 by 12 which equals $1,666 per month.

b) Annual income $_____ x 0.40 = $_____ divided by 12 = $_____ (principal; interest; tax; heating per month; 50 percent of monthly condo fee, if applicable; *plus* other loans)

Property taxes and heat along with the mortgage payment (and condo fees, if applicable) are used to ensure the borrower can afford the home at the minimum standards of living, based on the essential shelter costs of the property. The mortgage payment (principal and interest) are a given that the borrower must be able to afford; how-ever, property tax is also important as default can result in action by the city or municipality. Property tax liens have priority over the first mortgage. Monthly condominium/maintenance fees also take pre-cedence over a mortgage. Depending on whether or not the utilities of a given municipality are privatized or municipally owned, it is also possible that default of payment on utilities can result in a lien against the property that may take precedence over the mortgage. If the local utilities are municipally owned, this would be the case. If they are pri-vately owned, the company will send it to collections. This is essential-ly why a lender includes property tax, heating, and 50 percent of the monthly condo fee (if applicable) into the calculations to determine what the borrower qualifies to spend.

These ratios are general guidelines that lenders use to qualify and pre-approve you for a mortgage. However, some lenders are willing to approve a *conventional* borrower with a credit score of 680 or higher using a 44 percent TDS ratio. If you have 20 percent or more for a down payment, you are considered a conventional borrower and there will not be an insurance premium in most circumstances. Understand that a combination of your credit score, the amount of your down payment, and your employment are used to confirm and approve your mortgage loan. Again, lenders may have some discretion to slightly modify the ratios if you are a conventional borrower with a 680 or higher credit score. Speak to your mortgage professional regarding your individual mortgage situation.

Be careful about purchasing a vehicle, participating in long-term "don't pay" events for furniture or appliances, or incurring any other indebtedness because it may affect your TDS ratio. Always be aware of how borrowing will affect your credit score.

To finalize the maximum purchase price that you are able to spend you need to determine how much of a down payment you have, with 5 percent of the purchase price being a minimum amount. Again, if you have less than 20 percent down payment, you are considered a *high-ratio* borrower, and you will likely be required to obtain mortgage default insurance (also called mortgage loan insurance), which you will get from either CMHC or Genworth Financial Canada. This insurance does not protect the borrower, rather this insurance protects the lender against the borrower defaulting, thereby reducing the lender's exposure to loss. There is a one-time fee you pay for this insurance, due up front, and is subject to provincial sales tax where appropriate. If you do not have the money to pay this insurance premium, it is borrowed and added to your mortgage.

The fee varies depending on the down payment using the following guidelines:

- 5 percent down payment: Multiply the mortgage amount borrowed by 2.75 percent

- 10 percent down payment: Multiply the mortgage amount borrowed by 2 percent

- 15 percent down payment: Multiply the mortgage amount borrowed by 1.75 percent

Add 0.2 percent to each of the above scenarios if you decide to take a 30-year amortization.

Now take your total down payment amount and add this to the mortgage amount you qualify for. This amount equals your maximum purchase price. For example, if you qualify for a mortgage of $185,000 and your down payment is $15,000 ($185,000.00 + $15,000 = $200,000.00), the result is your maximum purchase price.

Occasionally, a buyer wants or needs a mortgage amount that is slightly higher than what the ratios allow, but due to other debt obligations (e.g., credit cards, student loans) that affect the ratios, the buyer simply doesn't qualify. Understand that I do not advocate or recommend that a buyer exceed his or her qualification limits; however, sometimes it is possible to find a lender that will allow a debt consolidation or similar program. Another option or necessity to free up money could be to pay off a loan or credit card completely. The less non-home related debt you have will result in more income available to qualify for a mortgage.

It is recommended that you speak with a mortgage professional about all the options, and carefully read the fine print. It is important to understand to what you are agreeing. Seek legal advice prior to signing *any* agreements.

3. How to Shop for a Mortgage and Get the Best Deal

Mortgages are products, and they have different terms and conditions. Don't be fooled into thinking that all mortgages are simple boilerplate documents that differ only by the interest rate offered. Break the mortgage into two components: the interest rate based on the length of the term, and the terms and conditions.

Your mortgage document is normally several pages in length and outlines the numerous terms and conditions. Different lenders can offer different terms and conditions and the interest rate may be negotiable. The key is finding the best mortgage for your needs, your long- and short-term goals, and a competitive interest rate.

Traditionally, borrowers obtain a mortgage pre-approval either directly from a bank or through a mobile mortgage representative or mortgage broker. If you choose to work with a specific bank, you may have the option of working with a mortgage representative located within a branch; some banks have "mobile" mortgage representatives that will meet with you outside the branch at a time and location convenient to your needs. Some mobile mortgage representatives also have offices located in real estate brokerages.

Bank mobile mortgage representatives are usually not salaried and, therefore, do not earn money unless they offer and you accept a mortgage from them. It is in their best interest to find and offer you a great deal. Being open to bundling other bank financial services and products may assist you in getting a better mortgage offer.

When dealing directly with a bank, don't forget that you are also dealing directly with the company that is lending the money (as opposed to dealing with a mortgage broker). How you present yourself to a bank can make a difference as to whether you obtain a mortgage and how good of a deal you are offered. Banks are interested in serving your financial needs — a mortgage is one product amongst several other financial products that they offer. You may be able to get a better mortgage deal if you are willing to use other financial products they offer such as bank accounts, credit cards, vehicle loan, insurance, RRSPs, and other investments.

In-branch bank staff normally work on a salaried basis, and often the mortgage representative can and will offer you a menu of other bank-related products and services. If you have an established relationship with a bank, especially if the branch staff know you personally, you might consider speaking with the mortgage representative to determine what he or she will offer. The mortgage representative will still need to go through an application process and will need to adhere to bank underwriting and risk assessment policies; however, having a personal banking relationship may help.

It is important to understand that if you go from bank to bank in an attempt to "shop" around for a mortgage, each prospective bank may do its own credit check, and this will affect your credit score as multiple hits or inquiries are recorded.

Mortgage professionals are also trained to work with the self-employed and new immigrants. This is a more specialized process. Some lenders offer specific mortgages and programs created specifically for self-employed people and new immigrants.

The mortgage market is competitive and mortgages are usually negotiable. Remember it is not only the interest rate that you may want to negotiate — terms such as prepayment privileges (on closed mortgages), portability options, early renewal, penalties, and a host of other options should be discussed.

Occasionally, lenders offer promotions for their mortgage products such as cash back, rate discounts, and prepayment options. It is important to assess the value and importance that their offerings have to your needs, or if you would prefer more of a no-frills mortgage. Be sure to read the fine print because occasionally special terms and offers carry specific rules that must be followed. Understand what the product is; don't simply choose a mortgage product based on the interest rate alone. Again, consult a lawyer prior to signing any contract or agreement.

It is a good idea to ask the mortgage broker or bank mortgage representative for an outline of all mortgage costs as well as an estimate of your mortgage payment (i.e., principal, interest, and taxes). Some will even help you prepare a housing budget.

3.1 Using the services of a mortgage broker

You also have the option of working with a mortgage broker — an independent licensed mortgage professional not directly employed or tied to one individual bank or lending institution. Depending on licensing, independent mortgage professionals are known by a few titles (e.g., mortgage broker, mortgage agent). For ease of clarity, an independent non-bank representative and non-bank mobile representative will be called a *mortgage broker.*

Most mortgage brokers work with a number of financial institutions, including banks, trust companies, insurance companies, and even private lenders. Mortgage brokers work on a commission basis. Their goal is to get you the best deal — a combination of interest rate and terms and conditions. Typically, the mortgage process with a mortgage broker involves you providing him or her with financial information (similar to what you would give to a bank representative) that he or she translates into a mortgage application. The mortgage broker will also need your permission to obtain your credit report. Most lenders will take the broker's credit report into their system (normally only one credit report is required); however lenders have their own "stale date" periods when they consider the credit report not usable, and a new one must be acquired. Discuss this with the mortgage broker in advance to minimize inquiries on your credit, which could affect your credit score.

Mortgage brokers understand the underwriting policy of the lenders, and generally know in advance how the lender will evaluate your application. His or her job is to put together your application, complete with the required financial information and documents, and present it to several prospective lenders. Once the mortgage application and data collection has been completed, a mortgage broker can shop for your mortgage using technology.

Your application can be sent electronically to a number of lenders, all of whom have the opportunity to review your application and determine if they will make a mortgage offer, and what kind. These individual lenders understand that other lenders are also reviewing and evaluating your application at the same time. If you look good on paper, the lenders will want your business.

Once all the mortgage offers are back (usually within 24 to 48 hours) you and your mortgage broker can review the offers and decide which mortgage is best for you. This allows you to select a mortgage product best suited to your individual financial needs.

Some lenders offer "performance" benefits to mortgage brokers, which can be a benefit to the home buyer. These same lenders assess the mortgage broker's volume of written mortgages, combined with their default and cancellation rate. When a mortgage broker acquires this status, he or she has the discretionary capability to give rate discounts below what is given to others.

Normally, as long as you are considered a good or "A" borrower, there is no additional out-of-pocket cost for the mortgage broker's service because he or she is paid by whatever lender you choose. Having said this, it is still recommended that prior to using the services of a mortgage broker you ask up front if there are any fees that you will need to pay for his or her services. More complicated or difficult mortgages, especially if private lenders are involved, may involve paying a mortgage broker fee. Get everything in writing.

Experienced, good mortgage brokers are knowledgeable about the products offered by most banks, trust companies, insurance companies, and private lenders, and are able to recommend a variety of different mortgage options for your consideration. Most mortgage brokers are very motivated and work hard to get their clients a good deal.

3.2 Mortgage term and interest rates

You will need to decide on both your amortization period (time frame to pay off the mortgage) and your mortgage term. Most first-time buyers choose a longer amortization (e.g., 25 or 30 years). Amortization length is usually the easy decision.

The term (or time frame for which you borrow the money at the interest rate you've agreed to) can be more difficult to decide upon. The shorter the time, the lower the interest rate and the greater the risk, as upon renewal, rates may have increased and it could cost you more to pay off your mortgage. With a low-interest rate environment, and the concern that rates may rise at some point in the future, many first-time buyers decide to lock in their interest rate for a longer term (often five, seven, or ten years), giving them the comfort and security that their mortgage payments will remain unchanged for a longer time frame. The attractive lower interest rate with shorter term mortgages comes with greater risk. You will need to determine your own risk tolerance and ability to carry and qualify for a higher rate mortgage upon renewal, if interest rates increase.

Regardless of which term you choose, and especially if you want a shorter term, some lenders, especially with respect to high-ratio borrowers (and depending on your credit score) will mandate a pre-approval using a longer term interest rate. Some lenders use an average of the five major Canadian banks' five-year *posted* interest rates to qualify a borrower. Other lenders use a five-year *discounted* variable rate. It depends on whether you are a conventional or high-ratio borrower, and what your credit score is. It varies and is up to the lender to decide. Of course, this plays a part in the underwriting criteria that a lender uses to determine the mortgage amount it will pre-approve. Your mortgage professional will discuss the criteria specific to your situation.

4. Plan Your Budget

Most first-time buyers have never experienced the costs associated with owning and maintaining a home and, for the most part, referring to mortgage amounts and numbers in the $300,000 to $400,000+ range can be a little intimidating and frightening. Of course, outside of your housing costs and potential other monthly liabilities (e.g., vehicle loan, student loan, credit cards), you also need to budget for day-to-day living expenses such as food, transportation, insurance, gas, clothing, entertainment, and savings.

Set up a budget that includes all of your anticipated living expenses in advance. Factor in what you expect to pay each month for mortgage, taxes, utilities, monthly strata or condominium/maintenance fees where applicable, and all other anticipated living expenses. Try using your budget for a few months.

You can use Worksheet 1 to help you create a monthly budget (this worksheet is also included on the CD). This way you will be able to track your spending and determine, prior to committing to a certain mortgage amount, how comfortable you will be. It will also enable you to decide if there are expenses or items that can be eliminated to reduce your spending (e.g., entertainment or travel).

It is not recommended that you become "house poor" and max out on credit cards or loans in order to make your monthly debt commitments — this is neither healthy nor fiscally responsible. Owning a home and building equity is a long-term plan that requires discipline and sacrifice. However, the long-term results are future security and building net worth. Many buyers decide to purchase for less than their maximum pre-qualification amount; they build in a "cushion" for unexpected expenses or life in general. This conservative approach is certainly something to consider. Remember: Short-term pain (and discipline) fosters long-term gain.

Worksheet 1
Monthly Budget

Estimate your monthly expenses. Itemize your spending each month and see how well you stay on track. Proper budgeting and money management will help with debt elimination and equity building.

Fixed income	$_____	
Other variable income	$_____	
Total Monthly Income	$_____	**(A)**

EXPENSES

Projected mortgage payment (P & I)	$_____	
Monthly property tax (projected)	$_____	
Monthly property insurance (estimate)	$_____	
Hydro (estimate)	$_____	
Gas (estimate)	$_____	
Water (estimate)	$_____	
Telephone/cell phone	$_____	
Cable	$_____	
Internet	$_____	
Condominium monthly fee (if applicable)	$_____	
Maintenance and repair	$_____	
Total Housing Expenses	$_____	**(B)**

OTHER EXPENSES

Groceries and toiletries	$_____	
Entertainment	$_____	
Clothing	$_____	
Child care	$_____	
Pet expenses	$_____	
Life insurance	$_____	
Other: _____	$_____	
Total Other Expenses	$_____	**(C)**

TRANSPORTATION EXPENSES

Gasoline	$_____	
Maintenance	$_____	
Insurance	$_____	
Parking	$_____	
Public transportation (e.g., bus, train)	$_____	
Total Transportation Expenses	$_____	**(D)**

LOANS AND CREDIT CARDS

Car loan payment	$_____	
Credit card (estimate)	$_____	
Other loan: _____	$_____	
Total Loans and Credit Cards	$_____	**(E)**

TOTAL EXPENSES (add B + C + D + E)	$_____	**(F)**

EXCESS INCOME AFTER EXPENSES

Income – Expenses (A minus F)	$_____

3

Eliminate Your Mortgage Fast

One of the reasons, other than lifestyle, that you may be considering the purchase of your first home is to build equity and net worth for the future. Real estate is a unique investment, and with prudent and disciplined money management you may be able to accomplish long-term security. Accelerating loan principal payments, if done correctly and consistently, can take on a whole new value.

1. Principal versus Interest

Mortgages typically have a 25- or 30-year amortization period and a shorter term (i.e., five, seven, or ten years). This means that your mortgage payment will remain the same for the duration of your term and the payments are calculated based on the length of the amortization. At the end of the term you will either renegotiate the term (which may have a different, possibly even higher interest rate, depending on the mortgage market at that time) or pay off the entire debt.

At the beginning of the mortgage, the principal versus interest allocation of the total mortgage payment is heavily skewed towards interest, with very little going towards paying off the outstanding principal debt. In essence, the mortgage is *front-loaded* with interest at the beginning of the mortgage. Over time, more of the mortgage payment is attributed towards the principal debt reduction and less is attributed towards interest.

For example, a 25-year amortized $250,000 mortgage with a 5 percent interest rate has a monthly mortgage payment of $1,454.01. If you multiply this amount by 60 (equivalent of 60 months or 5 years), you will have paid your lender approximately $87,241 in mortgage payments. The outstanding principal balance still owing after five years is $221,268.88! (See Sample 1 at the end of this chapter.)

The total paid over five years was approximately $87,241. Of that, roughly $28,731.12 went towards principal debt repayment and approximately $58,509.48 towards interest! It doesn't have to be this way.

As most mortgages (even closed mortgages) include an annual prepayment option percentage (normally 10 to 20 percent annually; this should be negotiated with your mortgage agreement), you should be allowed to make a prepayment of principal up to the allowable annual percentage of the original amount of your mortgage (i.e., 10 percent of a $200,000 mortgage = $20,000 annually or 15 percent of a $250,000 mortgage = $37,500 annually) of a prepayment of the principal debt each year without a penalty.

Of course, most homeowners do not have an extra $20,000 or $37,500 each year available to prepay against their mortgage principal debt. Even a small prepayment amount each year goes a long way to helping you accelerate through the mortgage amortization and save thousands in interest.

2. How to Pay off Your Mortgage Quickly

There are a couple of ways to help you pay off your mortgage quicker. One of the ways is to increase the amount of your regular payment whereby the increased amount is attributed directly towards principal debt reduction.

Another is to change your regular payments from monthly to biweekly, semimonthly, or weekly. This is known as an *accelerated* option. You can also make a prepayment of a lump sum amount in addition to your regular mortgage payment each payment period (i.e., monthly, biweekly, weekly). In any combination, all of these options work even faster.

If you simply arrange to pay your mortgage every two weeks instead of monthly you will reduce your amortization time frame. A

25-year amortization could be reduced by three and a half years just by paying biweekly as opposed to monthly!

When you pay monthly, you are making 12 monthly payments. By simply choosing to pay biweekly you are actually making 26 payments a year (there are 52 weeks in a year so divide by 2, and this equates to 26 biweekly payments). In effect, you are actually making an additional month's payment each year. This extra payment on a cumulative basis helps to accelerate you through the mortgage quicker, reduce the amortization time frame, as well as reduce the amount of interest you pay over the lifetime of your mortgage, since you have a mortgage for a shorter time frame.

That sounds easy enough to do and certainly worth the effort given the financial savings. If you find it convenient to pay your mortgage weekly (as opposed to biweekly or monthly) you will save even more money; however, the savings between biweekly and weekly are small compared to the huge difference between monthly and biweekly.

If you combine the biweekly or weekly payment option with one other option, you will be paying off the mortgage even quicker and saving more money in the process: a prepayment option. This is where the prepayment option that you hopefully negotiated or have included into your mortgage becomes important.

Assuming you have some sort of prepayment privilege, you will be allowed to prepay up to the percentage negotiated into your mortgage (e.g., 10 or 15 percent of the original mortgage amount) penalty-free each year. This additional prepayment amount will go straight towards principal debt reduction and, in turn, will help you pay off the mortgage faster and save you interest costs.

An easy way to manage your cash flow and keep track of prepayments made is to instruct your lender to take out an extra amount of money (amount predetermined) each payment along with your regular mortgage payment. For example, if your mortgage payment is $575 every two weeks, instruct your lender to deduct $625 every two weeks. That would equate to an extra $100 every month (four weeks). This equals $1,300 ($50 x 26 payments) a year. This may not sound like much; however, it adds up quickly, and the difference it makes saves you money in the long run! If your payment is automated, you don't have to do anything else — just ensure the correct amount is in your bank account.

When you increase payments this way you are allocating this additional prepayment towards the principal debt reduction which will affect the amount of interest you pay as you are paying off the mortgage principal debt sooner. The key is consistency. Make sure that this extra amount is deducted every payment, and when you can, increase it as much as possible.

Of course, throughout the year, if you find yourself with extra savings, a windfall, bonus, tax refund, or any other extra funds, consider paying it towards your principal debt. This in combination with biweekly payments and extra small prepayments (e.g., $50 extra each payment) can have astounding results on your mortgage. Remember, assuming it is allowed in your mortgage, you have a predetermined annual percentage prepayment allowed every year penalty-free against your mortgage. Most consumers do not reach their maximum allowance; however, it is important to understand that every little bit helps!

When you are negotiating your mortgage, ensure that you are allowed to make multiple prepayments throughout the year. Some mortgages require a minimum prepayment amount (e.g., $50). Some mortgages only allow a prepayment once a year on the anniversary date; while this helps, it is better to be allowed to make multiple prepayments throughout the year.

It is also easier if you automate this prepayment process. Speak with your lender about automatically deducting this extra prepayment routinely and applying it towards the principal debt reduction. Having this process set up with your lender in advance, accepting this as your payment, and budgeting for it will make a difference in the end.

Normally, once a year your lender will send you a mortgage summary outlining the amount paid towards both the interest and the principal debt, as well as the outstanding principal debt balance. This should motivate you to continue with the goal of paying off your mortgage faster while building equity and net worth for yourself and your family.

3. Your Mortgage Term

Let's review the mortgage term and how this affects your mortgage payments. With interest rates currently at affordable levels (as of the writing of this book) and expected to increase at some point, you may want to consider setting up a fixed five-year or longer term mortgage. The interest rate will be somewhat higher on a longer term mortgage than a shorter one-, two-, or three-year term; you will need to weigh the pros and cons of locking in an interest rate for a longer period of time. This will not only give you the peace of mind that your mortgage payment will remain the same for an extended period of time, but it can also assist you with the accelerated payment plan since you will be able to budget more effectively.

Most homeowners are drawn to a shorter term mortgage due to the lower interest rate which of course makes the mortgage payment more affordable. Where the problem lies is:

1. Should interest rates rise, upon renewal what will you do if the renewal interest rate increases, thereby also increasing your mortgage payment? Some homeowners need to increase their amortization time frame (assuming they are not already extended to the maximum) to help lower their regular mortgage payment so they aren't house poor. This adds more interest over the lifetime of the mortgage and certainly does not help with paying off the mortgage quicker.

2. What will you do if you are already extended to the maximum on the amortization and don't re-qualify (based on GDS and TDS ratios) to renew your mortgage at the increased rates? This could create a problem. Perhaps you will need to find a co-signer or sell your home, and quickly.

Borrowing rules can change. In Canada, for many years the maximum amortization period was 25 years; however, sometime in the mid-2000s the maximum amortization period crept up to 40 years! This made qualifying for and carrying a mortgage easier, but it also added tens of thousands of dollars of interest to the life of your mortgage and kept homeowners with a mortgage in debt longer. In 2010, it was decided to decrease the maximum amortization period to 35 years, and then again in 2011, it was reduced to 30 years (for most borrowers). Could it be reduced back to 25 years? Who knows?

If you began your mortgage with a longer 30-, 35-, or 40-year amortization period and took a shorter term (meaning renewal will be sooner), this may change what you qualify for and your monthly cash flow if interest rates have increased on renewal. You can see how dramatically different your financial picture could look. More importantly, will you qualify to renew your mortgage at the end of your term?

As mentioned earlier, mortgages are often front-loaded with interest. Many homeowners opt for a shorter term (with lower interest rates), and when they renew (assuming they re-qualify) if interest rates have increased, they take the same amortization period (unless they are forced to take a shorter amortization due to rule changes). The problem is, if you don't decrease the amortization period to be less than the amount of time you have already been paying your mortgage (e.g., decreasing the amortization from 30 years to 25 years if you have had the home for 5 years), upon renewal, you are front-loading the interest on your renewal again. Upon renewal, given that the mortgage is front-loaded with interest, you are renewing for almost the same amount as you began with! Even worse, some homeowners who have enjoyed appreciation in the value of their home decide to put a line of credit on their home and borrow money against it to purchase vehicles, take holidays, and to buy or do a host of other things, resulting in adding more debt to their property — all the while adding more interest to their mortgage. The lesson here is if your home appreciates in value, don't use your home's increase in value as a source of funds (similar to an ATM), because this spells trouble.

Real estate values can move in cycles. If the real estate market experiences a pullback that results in a decline in property values, you may find yourself over-leveraged against the home's value. If this occurs during your mortgage renewal time, you may find it difficult if not impossible to find a lender who will lend or renew your mortgage for greater than a percentage (e.g., 95 percent) of the actual value of the property at that time. Now what do you do? If you decide to sell your home, you may have negative equity and will owe the bank the difference. You will also have to find a place to live.

Wise mortgage planning involves borrowing at a level that you feel comfortable that you can manage, and setting up a mortgage acceleration payment plan to pay off your mortgage debt quicker. Remember, short-term pain can mean long-term gain!

Try to look at appreciation on the home (which may or may not occur) as a bonus. Consider purchasing a home with a mortgage debt that is comfortable and realistic to manage, and focus on building equity through accelerated debt reduction. Remember, real estate is an investment and one that can provide many benefits, but as with any investment there are risks and responsibilities. Being prepared and knowledgeable about your options and consequences in advance will enable you to make appropriate decisions.

4. Begin with a Starter Home

There is the risk that the value of your home may decline (as with any investment, risk exists). At some point in the future you may decide that you want or need to trade up to a larger and more expensive home; if you have equity in your existing home this can help you. Keep in mind that the higher you go in price, normally the fewer the number of buyers exist; more consumers can afford $200,000 than $400,000, and more can afford $500,000 than $800,000. The point is, the higher the price range the fewer the number of buyers available and capable of that kind of spending.

How does this relate to you? If you automate your prepayment with additional principal each payment period and consistently work towards paying off the mortgage quicker, you will be building equity; you will need equity (as the down payment) on another real estate purchase which you would get from the sale of the existing home should you decide to trade up to another. Generally speaking, when there is a decline in real estate values, more expensive homes decline on a greater percentage basis than more affordable homes. For example, a $600,000 home may decline 20 percent in value, whereas a starter home may decline 10 to 12 percent. This is due to the fact that value is derived from supply and demand.

The more affordable starter home will likely always have more willing and capable buyers than a more expensive home; thus, the decline in the starter home's cost may be less. As long as you have equity in your home and can qualify to carry a larger mortgage, this could work to your benefit as the trade-up home's value may have declined more than your existing starter home's value. In other words, the spread between the pricing on the starter home and the more expensive home may be narrower. Having equity in your existing home is important, so try to work on accelerating through the amortization schedule and eliminating the mortgage debt faster.

5. Pay off Your Mortgage Faster

Now that you have an understanding of how important term and amortization are and how they are tied to one another in the big picture, consider setting up your mortgage using the following plan (or a variation of it):

Begin with a 25-year amortization. Review Sample 2, which has a $250,000 mortgage with a five-year accelerated fixed rate of 5 percent. The monthly mortgage payment is $1,454.01 and the biweekly payment is $727.01.

If you simply pay this mortgage biweekly, the amortization will shrink from 650 biweekly payments to approximately 559 biweekly payments (based on a 25-year amortization). Now let's set up a plan to pay off this mortgage early and save tens of thousands of dollars of interest.

Assuming your mortgage comes with a 15 or 20 percent prepayment option (which most do), instruct your lender to increase your mortgage payment by $50 every biweekly payment (or approximately $100 per month), with this amount going straight towards principal debt reduction. Look at the difference in the examples:

Sample 1 illustrates the outstanding balance after five years (i.e., 60 payments) is approximately $221,268.88 (assuming you paid monthly and made no increase in your monthly mortgage payment) of which approximately $58,509.45 is interest during the first five years. Keep in mind this also means that when you renew your mortgage, the renewal amount is approximately $221,268.88 which is not much less than you initially borrowed. Let's hope interest rates have not increased dramatically at renewal, as this could substantially affect your cash flow.

Sample 3 outlines the outstanding balance after five years (i.e., 130 payments), which is approximately $205,554.32 if you paid your mortgage biweekly and added $50.00 per biweekly payment. This equates to an extra $1,300.00 per year ($50.00 x 26 payments = $1,300.00). The interest is approximately $56,565.62. The renewal amount is much less at approximately $205,554.32 than in Sample 1.

Sample 4 shows the outstanding balance of approximately $198,188.49 after five years if you paid your mortgage biweekly and added $100.00 per biweekly payment which equates to an extra $2,600.00 per year ($100.00 x 26 payments = $2,600.00). The interest is roughly $55,699.79. You can see how fast this adds up. This is the power of compounding!

When you renew your mortgage after five years, your renewal balance is substantially less in Sample 4 than in Sample 1. This adds a buffer for you should rates increase. Upon renewal of your mortgage you should consider reducing the amortization period by at least five years (time that you have already spent paying a mortgage) as this will help to accelerate you through your mortgage. Of course, you will still need to qualify for the new mortgage on renewal. Having lower outstanding mortgage debt on renewal will help you re-qualify should interest rates increase.

Many homeowners keep the same amortization period as they began with each renewal, only to find that it takes them longer to pay off the mortgage. Carefully consider what the future may hold for interest rates. Most economists and professionals will agree that the potential for interest rates to increase at some point in the future is likely. Factor this into your long-term financial plans.

On renewal, if you shorten the amortization period to 20 years (from the original 25 years) and your renewal balance is approximately $198,188.49 (as in Sample 4), continue paying biweekly (to shorten the amortization) and continue to add $50 or $100 (or whatever you can afford) to each biweekly payment.

It is difficult to predict what the interest rate will be five years from now. If you consistently continue with this plan, your mortgage will be paid off sooner and you will save money that would have been attributed towards interest.

The interest on your principal residence mortgage is normally not tax deductible; in other words, you are probably paying your mortgage with after-tax dollars. (Check with your tax or accounting professionals to determine if this is your situation.) Paying off your mortgage quickly will build equity through mortgage debt elimination. Consider any value appreciation, should this occur, as a bonus. This is a very good position to be in and certainly worth the time to set up your accelerated mortgage reduction plan sooner rather than later.

Some homeowners opt to take a 10-year term (instead of a 5-year term) and a 25-year amortization. When rates are low, despite the higher rate you pay on a 10-year term versus a 5-year term, the stability and comfort that come with not having to worry about renewing a mortgage for 10 years is something to consider. It is possible that over 10 years you will have an increase in income and you will have had more time to pay down mortgage debt. Stay focused and disciplined; in the end it will pay off for you.

It is unbelievable how an additional $50 or $100 regular prepayment towards the principal debt makes over the life of your mortgage. To help motivate you to stay on track and disciplined, consider the corresponding interest that is attached to each $50- or $100-payment. Every additional prepayment saves you some interest and cumulatively over time, will save you a lot of interest and time on your mortgage. Do the math because it really adds up.

Once you pay off your mortgage, you will have a feeling of security and you will have the additional disposable income each month that would have been allocated towards your mortgage, to spend or invest however you wish.

Once your mortgage is paid off, you have equity, regardless of whether the value of the property has appreciated or not. Keep in mind that you may also be able to tap into your equity for investment purposes (e.g., to buy a rental or income property, or a business). If you borrow equity from your home for investment purposes, this loan or mortgage may become tax deductible. Consult with a tax, accounting, or legal professional for advice specific to your needs and individual situation.

This is one way to accumulate other assets in real estate. Take it one step at a time. It is imperative that you begin with a good plan, a solid foundation, and work towards paying off the mortgage quickly.

So what happens if you move during the first ten years of ownership? This happens all the time; that's why most mortgages are portable. However, each time you move or change your mortgage, technically the mortgage needs to be re-qualified. Many homeowners don't realize this; if you have had a change in employment or life circumstances, the lender will need to re-evaluate your mortgage and determine your qualifications. Prior to making any major changes, don't take for granted that you already have a mortgage because it may not be the case that you can simply take it with you.

Mortgage rules may change, so contact your lender or mortgage professional to find out the details and how current rules may affect your mortgage.

Hopefully you see the benefits to accelerating through your mortgage and paying off the debt quicker. The key is proper planning at the beginning and staying disciplined.

Sample 1
Mortgage for 25 Years

Principal: $250,000
Interest Rate: 5.0%
Amortization: 25 years
Payment Term: 5 years

Payment Method: Monthly
Accelerated: N/A
Anniversary Amount:
Payment Amount: $1,454.01

Payment	Date	Interest	Principal	Remaining Principal
1	08/15/2011	$1,030.98	$423.03	$249,576.97
2	09/15/2011	$1,029.23	$424.78	$249,152.19
3	10/15/2011	$1,027.48	$426.53	$248,725.66
4	11/15/2011	$1,025.72	$428.29	$248,297.37
5	12/15/2011	$1,023.96	$430.05	$247,867.32
6	01/15/2012	$1,022.18	$431.83	$247,435.49
7	02/15/2012	$1,020.40	$433.61	$247,001.88
8	03/15/2012	$1,018.61	$435.40	$246,566.48
9	04/15/2012	$1,016.82	$437.19	$246,129.29
10	05/15/2012	$1,015.02	$438.99	$245,690.30
11	06/15/2012	$1,013.21	$440.80	$245,249.50
12	07/15/2012	$1,011.39	$442.62	$244,806.88
13	08/15/2012	$1,009.56	$444.45	$244,362.43
14	09/15/2012	$1,007.73	$446.28	$243,916.15
15	10/15/2012	$1,005.89	$448.12	$243,468.03
16	11/15/2012	$1,004.04	$449.97	$243,018.06
17	12/15/2012	$1,002.19	$451.82	$242,566.24
18	01/15/2013	$1,000.32	$453.69	$242,112.55
19	02/15/2013	$998.45	$455.56	$241,656.99
20	03/15/2013	$996.57	$457.44	$241,199.55
21	04/15/2013	$994.69	$459.32	$240,740.23
22	05/15/2013	$992.79	$461.22	$240,279.01
23	06/15/2013	$990.89	$463.12	$239,815.89
24	07/15/2013	$988.98	$465.03	$239,350.86
25	08/15/2013	$987.06	$466.95	$238,883.91
26	09/15/2013	$985.14	$468.87	$238,415.04
27	10/15/2013	$983.20	$470.81	$237,944.23
28	11/15/2013	$981.26	$472.75	$237,471.48
29	12/15/2013	$979.31	$474.70	$236,996.78
30	01/15/2014	$977.35	$476.66	$236,520.12
31	02/15/2014	$975.39	$478.62	$236,041.50
32	03/15/2014	$973.42	$480.59	$235,560.91
33	04/15/2014	$971.43	$482.58	$235,078.33
34	05/15/2014	$969.44	$484.57	$234,593.76
35	06/15/2014	$967.44	$486.57	$234,107.19
36	07/15/2014	$965.44	$488.57	$233,618.62
37	08/15/2014	$963.42	$490.59	$233,128.03
38	09/15/2014	$961.40	$492.61	$232,635.42
39	10/15/2014	$959.37	$494.64	$232,140.78
40	11/15/2014	$957.33	$496.68	$231,644.10

Sample 1 — Continued

41	12/15/2014	$955.28	$498.73	$231,145.37
42	01/15/2015	$953.22	$500.79	$230,644.58
43	02/15/2015	$951.16	$502.85	$230,141.73
44	03/15/2015	$949.09	$504.92	$229,636.81
45	04/15/2015	$947.00	$507.01	$229,129.80
46	05/15/2015	$944.91	$509.10	$228,620.70
47	06/15/2015	$942.81	$511.20	$228,109.50
48	07/15/2015	$940.70	$513.31	$227,596.19
49	08/15/2015	$938.59	$515.42	$227,080.77
50	09/15/2015	$936.46	$517.55	$226,563.22
51	10/15/2015	$934.33	$519.68	$226,043.54
52	11/15/2015	$932.18	$521.83	$225,521.71
53	12/15/2015	$930.03	$523.98	$224,997.73
54	01/15/2016	$927.87	$526.14	$224,471.59
55	02/15/2016	$925.70	$528.31	$223,943.28
56	03/15/2016	$923.52	$530.49	$223,412.79
57	04/15/2016	$921.34	$532.67	$222,880.12
58	05/15/2016	$919.14	$534.87	$222,345.25
59	06/15/2016	$916.93	$537.08	$221,808.17
60	07/15/2016	$914.72	$539.29	$221,268.88*
	Total	$58,509.48	$28,731.12	

Samples 1–4 used with permission from The Mortgage Centre/ R.D.M. Financial Consultants.

Sample 2
Mortgage with Monthly and Biweekly Payments
for 25 Years

Principal: 250,000
Interest Rate: 5.0%
Amortization: 25 years
Start Date: 07/15/2011

Term: 5 years
Payment Method: Monthly*
Accelerated: Yes
Payment Amount: $1,454.01

Payment	Date	Interest	Principal
1	08/15/2011	$1,030.98	$423.03
2	09/15/2011	$1,029.23	$424.78
3	10/15/2011	$1,027.48	$426.53
4	11/15/2011	$1,025.72	$428.29
5	12/15/2011	$1,023.96	$430.05
6	01/15/2012	$1,022.18	$431.83
7	02/15/2012	$1,020.40	$433.61
8	03/15/2012	$1,018.61	$435.40
9	04/15/2012	$1,016.82	$437.19
10	05/15/2012	$1,015.02	$438.99
11	06/15/2012	$1,013.21	$440.80

Principal: 250,000
Interest Rate: 5.0%
Amortization: 25 years
Start Date: 07/15/2011

Term: 5 years
Payment Method: Biweekly*
Accelerated: Yes
Payment Amount: $727.01

Payment	Date	Interest	Principal
1	07/29/2011	$475.31	$251.70
2	08/12/2011	$474.83	$252.18
3	08/26/2011	$474.35	$252.66
4	09/09/2011	$473.87	$253.14
5	09/23/2011	$473.39	$253.62
6	10/07/2011	$472.91	$254.10
7	10/21/2011	$472.42	$254.59
8	11/04/2011	$471.94	$255.07
9	11/18/2011	$471.46	$255.55
10	12/02/2011	$470.97	$256.04
11	12/16/2011	$470.48	$256.53

Sample 3
Mortgage with Biweekly Payments Plus $50 for 25 Years

Principal: $250,000
Interest Rate: 5.0%
Amortization: 25 years
Payment Term: 5 years

Payment Method: Biweekly
Accelerated: Yes
Anniversary Amount:
Payment Amount: $777.01 (added $50)

Payment	Date	Interest	Principal	Remaining Principal
1	07/29/2011	$475.31	$301.70	$249,698.30
2	08/12/2011	$474.74	$302.27	$249,396.03
3	08/28/2011	$474.16	$302.85	$249,093.18
4	09/09/2011	$473.59	$303.42	$248,789.76
5	09/23/2011	$473.01	$304.00	$248,485.76
6	10/07/2011	$472.43	$304.58	$248,181.18
7	10/21/2011	$471.85	$305.16	$247,876.02
8	11/04/2011	$471.27	$305.74	$247,570.28
9	11/18/2011	$470.69	$306.32	$247,263.96
10	12/02/2011	$470.11	$306.90	$246,957.06
11	12/16/2011	$469.52	$307.49	$246,649.57
12	12/30/2011	$468.94	$308.07	$246,341.50
13	01/13/2012	$468.35	$308.66	$246,032.84
14	01/27/2012	$467.77	$309.24	$245,723.60
15	02/10/2012	$467.18	$309.83	$245,413.77
16	02/24/2012	$466.59	$310.42	$245,103.35
17	03/09/2012	$466.00	$311.01	$244,792.34
18	03/23/2012	$465.41	$311.60	$244,480.74
19	04/06/2012	$464.82	$312.19	$244,168.55
20	04/20/2012	$464.22	$312.79	$243,855.76
21	05/04/2012	$463.63	$313.38	$243,542.38
22	05/18/2012	$463.03	$313.98	$243,228.40
23	06/01/2012	$462.43	$314.58	$242,913.82
24	06/15/2012	$461.84	$315.17	$242,598.65
25	06/29/2012	$461.24	$315.77	$242,282.88
26	07/13/2012	$460.64	$316.37	$241,966.51
27	07/27/2012	$460.04	$316.97	$241,649.54
28	08/10/2012	$459.43	$317.58	$241,331.96
29	08/24/2012	$458.83	$318.18	$241,013.78
30	09/07/2012	$458.22	$318.79	$240,694.99
31	09/21/2012	$457.62	$319.39	$240,375.60
32	10/05/2012	$457.01	$320.00	$240,055.60
33	10/19/2012	$456.40	$320.61	$239,734.99
34	11/02/2012	$455.79	$321.22	$239,413.77
35	11/16/2012	$455.18	$321.83	$239,091.94
36	11/30/2012	$454.57	$322.44	$238,769.50
37	12/14/2012	$453.96	$323.05	$238,446.45
38	12/28/2012	$453.34	$323.67	$238,122.78

Sample 3 — Continued

39	01/11/2013	$452.73	$324.28	$237,798.50
40	01/25/2013	$452.11	$324.90	$237,473.60
41	02/08/2013	$451.49	$325.52	$237,148.08
42	02/22/2013	$450.87	$326.14	$236,821.94
43	03/08/2013	$450.25	$326.76	$236,495.18
44	03/22/2013	$449.63	$327.38	$236,167.80
45	04/05/2013	$449.01	$328.00	$235,839.80
46	04/19/2013	$448.39	$328.62	$235,511.18
47	05/03/2013	$447.76	$329.25	$235,181.93
48	05/17/2013	$447.14	$329.87	$234,852.06
123	04/01/2016	$396.63	$380.38	$208,237.30
124	04/15/2016	$395.91	$381.10	$207,856.20
125	04/29/2016	$395.18	$381.83	$207,474.37
126	05/13/2016	$394.46	$382.55	$207,091.82
127	05/27/2016	$393.73	$383.28	$206,708.54
128	06/10/2016	$393.00	$384.01	$206,324.53
129	06/24/2016	$392.27	$384.74	$205,939.79
130	07/08/2016	$391.54	$385.47	$205,554.32*
	Total	$56,565.62	$44,445.68	

Sample 4
Mortgage with Biweekly Payments Plus $100 for 25 Years

Principal: $250,000
Interest Rate: 5.0%
Amortization: 25 years
Payment Term: 5 years

Payment Method: Biweekly
Accelerated: Yes
Anniversary Amount:
Payment Amount: $827.01 (added $100)

Payment	Date	Interest	Principal	Remaining Principal
1	07/29/2011	$475.31	$351.70	$249,648.30
2	08/12/2011	$474.64	$352.37	$249,295.93
3	08/26/2011	$473.97	$353.04	$248,942.89
4	09/09/2011	$473.30	$353.71	$248,589.18
5	09/23/2011	$472.63	$354.38	$248,234.80
6	10/07/2011	$471.95	$355.06	$247,879.74
7	10/21/2011	$471.28	$355.73	$247,524.01
8	11/04/2011	$470.60	$356.41	$247,167.60
9	11/18/2011	$469.92	$357.09	$246,810.51
10	12/02/2011	$469.25	$357.76	$246,452.75
11	12/16/2011	$468.57	$358.44	$246,094.31
12	12/30/2011	$467.88	$359.13	$245,735.18
13	01/13/2012	$467.20	$359.81	$245,375.37
14	01/27/2012	$466.52	$360.49	$245,014.88
15	02/10/2012	$465.83	$361.18	$244,653.70
16	02/24/2012	$465.14	$361.87	$244,291.83
17	03/09/2012	$464.46	$362.55	$243,929.28
18	03/23/2012	$463.77	$363.24	$243,566.04
19	04/06/2012	$463.08	$363.93	$243,202.11
20	04/20/2012	$462.38	$364.63	$242,837.48
21	05/04/2012	$461.69	$365.32	$242,472.16
22	05/18/2012	$461.00	$366.01	$242,106.15
23	06/01/2012	$460.30	$366.71	$241,739.44
24	06/15/2012	$459.60	$367.41	$241,372.03
25	06/29/2012	$458.91	$368.10	$241,003.93
26	07/13/2012	$458.21	$368.80	$240,635.13
27	07/27/2012	$457.50	$369.51	$240,265.62
28	08/10/2012	$456.80	$370.21	$239,895.41
29	08/24/2012	$456.10	$370.91	$239,524.50
30	09/07/2012	$455.39	$371.62	$239,152.88
31	09/21/2012	$454.69	$372.32	$238,780.56
32	10/05/2012	$453.98	$373.03	$238,407.53
33	10/19/2012	$453.27	$373.74	$238,033.79
34	11/02/2012	$452.56	$374.45	$237,659.34
35	11/16/2012	$451.85	$375.16	$237,284.18
36	11/30/2012	$451.13	$375.88	$236,908.30
37	12/14/2012	$450.42	$376.59	$236,531.71
38	12/28/2012	$449.70	$377.31	$236,154.40
39	01/11/2013	$448.99	$378.02	$235,776.38
40	01/25/2013	$448.27	$378.74	$235,397.64

Sample 4 — Continued

41	02/08/2013	$447.55	$379.46	$235,018.18
42	02/22/2013	$446.83	$380.18	$234,638.00
43	03/08/2013	$446.10	$380.91	$234,257.09
44	03/22/2013	$445.38	$381.63	$233,875.46
45	04/05/2013	$444.65	$382.36	$233,493.10
46	04/19/2013	$443.93	$383.08	$233,110.02
47	05/03/2013	$443.20	$383.81	$232,726.21
48	05/17/2013	$442.47	$384.54	$232,341.67
126	05/13/2016	$381.06	$445.95	$199,980.79
127	05/27/2016	$380.21	$446.80	$199,533.99
128	06/10/2016	$379.36	$447.65	$199,086.34
129	06/24/2016	$378.51	$448.50	$198,637.84
130	07/03/2016	$377.66	$449.35	$198,188.49*
	Total	$55,699.79	$51,811.51	

Note: The sample amortization charts were issued for example purposes. Every effort was made to ensure the numbers were accurate.

4

Government Programs

R eal estate is a big part of Canadian life. Tens of thousands of Canadians work in the industry as developers, architects, surveyors, builders, contractors, and labourers. There are municipal, city, and other government personnel; utility and other home-related services; real estate professionals; lawyers; bank employees; mortgage and insurance professionals; and accounting professionals. Add to that employees of ancillary industries such as home furnishings, appliances, maintenance, and home retail stores.

Housing is not only a need, it is also a large component of the financial health of the economy. Because of this, governments offer housing related programs which make it easier for consumers to buy and afford homes. Being aware of and understanding these programs can save you money on your purchase and help make it more affordable.

1. The 5 Percent Down Payment Program

When you purchase a home, you will need a down payment. Many first-time buyers become understandably confused and think that they need 20 to 30 percent of the purchase price as a down payment before they can purchase their first home. Usually this is not the case (although some exceptions exist so check with your lender).

The potential confusion is sometimes caused by not understanding that two categories of mortgage financing exist (i.e., conventional and high ratio financing). It's important to understand the difference between the two categories. While having a large down payment is a good thing, for most buyers it is unrealistic.

How much do you need for a down payment? What resources do you have to get the down payment? With the costs of everyday living expenses, saving for a home can be difficult. A number of consumers have the income to qualify to afford a monthly mortgage payment, but they don't have a large down payment to be able to acquire a conventional mortgage (i.e., one with 20 percent or more down payment). Fortunately, you may not require such a large down payment; you may be able to qualify as a *high ratio* borrower with a smaller down payment requirement.

Canada's 5 percent Down Payment Program enables qualified home buyers to purchase a home with 5 percent of the purchase price as the down payment. You can put down more than 5 percent; however, 5 percent is the minimum. If your purchase price budget is $250,000, this equates to $12,500 for a down payment. You will still need to save or acquire this amount of money; however, it is more attainable than saving or acquiring 20 to 30 percent of the purchase price.

With high-ratio financing, the lender usually requires that the borrower pay for *mortgage default insurance* (also known as mortgage loan insurance) to protect the lender against mortgage default. Canada Mortgage and Housing Corporation (CMHC) as well as Genworth Financial Canada provide mortgage default insurance. Visit them at www.cmhc.ca and www.genworth.ca.

The 5 percent Down Payment Program is available to all (not just first-time) buyers and has been available for a number of years. It has helped tens of thousands of buyers purchase a home. There are rules and requirements to qualify for the 5 percent Down Payment Program:

- You need to save 5 percent of the purchase price or appraised price — whichever is lower. This program applies to single-family and two-unit dwellings. You will need to show copies of your bank statements to show that the money has been in your account for some time. In other words, you have to prove that you have it.

Examples of acceptable sources of down payment include savings accounts, RRSPs, funds borrowed against proven assets, or a gift from an immediate relative that you do not have to pay back. If the down payment is a gift (as opposed to a loan), you will need to confirm that it was a gift and does not need to be repaid. Often, the lender asks for a letter from the gift giver stating that it is a gift. A down payment as a gift from an immediate family member is normally acceptable for the purchase of single-family or two-unit dwellings.

Possible other sources of down payment, such as borrowed funds and lender incentives (i.e., cash back) may also be acceptable, provided the funds are at arm's length. Your lender will confirm the qualifying criteria.

- Gross Debt Service Ratio (GDS) and Total Debt Service Ratio (TDS) — the total of Principal, Interest, Property tax, and Heating (PITH) as well as land or site leases (if applicable) cannot be greater than 32 percent of your gross income. If you are considering a condominium, you will also need to include 50 percent of the condominium fee into this calculation.

  The money spent on PITH as well as land or site lease (if applicable) and 50 percent of the condominium fee where applicable, as well as all other debt payments (e.g., credit cards, vehicle loans) cannot be greater than 40 percent of your total income (TDS).

- The home must be located in Canada and it must be available and suitable to live in year-round. Additionally, the home, or at least one unit of the dwelling, must be intended for occupancy, rent free at some time during the year by the borrower or a relative of the borrower.

- The program is only available to permanent residents of Canada.

- In addition to the 5 percent down payment, you will need to budget for additional closing costs which can range between 1.5 percent and 4 percent of the purchase price to cover costs such as legal fees, land transfer tax, and title insurance. The 5 percent down payment program allows you to borrow money to cover your closing costs; however, if you do so, you will need to factor the repayment of the closing costs loan into the debt service ratios (TDS).

There are a few lenders that offer mortgage programs or products that offer cash back and some buyers use this money to pay for closing costs. I am in no way endorsing or not endorsing the "cash back" mortgage program, I'm simply informing you of this option. It is prudent to review all options and weigh the pros and cons of all your choices with a short- and long-term viewpoint. It is important that you are aware and understand all the terms, conditions, and your responsibilities with respect to lender-sponsored cash back and other programs as they may include specific restrictions and fees or responsibilities that you need to adhere to. If you are unsure, or unaware, of all the details ask and obtain legal advice. Remember to get everything in writing.

- The loan insurance premium is calculated as a percentage of the loan amount and is based on your down payment. For example, if your down payment is 5 percent, you will be paying an insurer's fee of 2.75 percent of the mortgage amount, which can be paid when the mortgage is advanced or, it can be included in the amount that you owe on the mortgage and paid with your mortgage payment. Non-traditional down payments (i.e., line of credit, cash back) will incur a slightly higher premium of 2.9 percent of the mortgage amount.

  In some provinces, such as Ontario, the 2.75 percent fee is considered an insurance premium and is subject to provincial sales tax which is payable in full on closing and cannot be added to the mortgage amount. Be sure to budget for this expense. Double check with your province to determine, in advance, if there is a tax added to the fee and include this in your budget.

- If you put down more than the minimum 5 percent down payment, the insurance premium is less than the 2.75 percent. It is on a sliding scale. For example:

  - 85.01 to 90 percent: the premium is 2 percent[*]

  - 80.01 to 85 percent: the premium is 1.75 percent[*]

  Should you move homes in the future and wish to "port" your existing mortgage, check with your lender and lawyer as the criteria, especially for high-ratio borrowers, may affect how you qualify and may involve additional premiums. Once

---

[*] **Note:** Add 0.2 percent to all premiums if you opt for a 30-year amortization period.

again, get everything is writing and when in doubt ask, and seek appropriate legal advice from your lawyer.

- Canada Mortgage and Housing Corporation (CMHC) has a program that offers loan insurance refunds for homeowners who purchase an energy-efficient home or purchase and make energy-saving renovations to an existing home.

Rules change often. Check with your lender on the exact premium amount as well as for detailed information about specific programs to meet your individual needs, and get everything in writing! Contact CMHC or Genworth Financial Canada for additional details.

2. Home Buyers' Plan

Canada's Home Buyers' Plan (HBP) is a popular plan that enables home buyers to access their Registered Retirement Savings Plan (RRSP) money to use towards a down payment and closing costs (from Canada Revenue Agency, www.cra-arc.gc.ca, accessed October, 2011).

The HBP is a program in which you can withdraw up to $25,000 tax-free from your RRSP to buy or build a qualifying home for yourself or for a related person with a disability. You are required to repay this money into your RRSP, generally by yearly payments for up to 15 years. If two people purchase a home together (e.g., husband and wife) and both qualify under the program, they may be able to double the amount to $50,000. If you don't repay what you are supposed to in a given year, the missed amount will be included in your income and you will be taxed on it.

To qualify, you will need to meet HBP rules and conditions:

- You need to be a first-time home buyer. CRA is specific on the definition of a first-time buyer. You do not qualify as a first-time buyer if you or your spouse or common-law partner owned and occupied a home as your principal residence in the past five years. CRA determines the past five years as the time frame from "January 1 of the fourth year before the year of withdrawal and ending 31 days before your withdrawal." For clarity, or if you are close to the cutoff dates, or you are unsure, contact CRA for your own specific timing details.

  Exceptions to this rule exist if you are disabled, or you are buying or building a home for a related person with a disability. Visit CRA's website at www.cra-arc.gc.ca for additional details.

- The home itself must qualify; it must be in Canada, and it can be a single-family dwelling; semidetached; townhouse; mobile home; condominium; apartment in a duplex, triplex, fourplex; or apartment buildings.

- The funds are required to be in your RRSP for at least 90 days before withdrawal.

- It must be your intention to occupy the home as your principal residence, and not later than one year after buying or building the home. This also applies if you buy or build a home that qualifies for a related person with a disability, meaning the intention must be for that person to occupy the home as a principal residence.

- Before you can withdraw funds you need to have entered into a written agreement to build or buy a qualifying residence (i.e., an agreement of purchase and sale) and it must be bought or built for yourself or fall under the "related person with disability" rules.

- The withdrawal limit is $25,000. You can only take the money out of an RRSP if you are the beneficiary, and you can withdraw from more than one RRSP as long as you are the plan owner of each RRSP. Your spouse has to follow the same rules and can withdraw up to $25,000 tax-free from his or her RRSP of which he or she is the beneficiary to put towards the same home. Common-law spouses are defined as spouses who have lived together continuously for at least 12 months. If the common-law spouses are natural or adoptive parents of a child, the 12-month continuous cohabitation requirement may be overlooked. This means that a total of $50,000 ($25,000 from each spouse's plan) can be put towards the same home.

- There are rules with respect to timing; you are required to receive all the withdrawals in the same calendar year. Ask the CRA about time lines.

- You or your spouse or common-law partner or related person that qualifies with a disability cannot own the qualifying home more than 30 days before the RRSP withdrawal is made.

- Check the type of RRSP you have as you may not be able to withdraw funds from a locked-in RRSP or a group RRSP. For greater clarity, obtain approval from CRA as to whether this applies to your situation.

- Upon receipt of your withdrawal funds until the time a qualifying home is built or purchased you must be a Canadian resident. If after a qualifying home is bought or built you become a nonresident, your withdrawal may still be eligible; however, there may be special rules for the repayment of the balance. Ensure you understand your responsibilities and the rules.

- If you own co-op shares that entitle you to occupy and also give you an equity interest in a housing unit in Canada, this also qualifies. Co-op shares that only provide the right to tenancy in the housing do not qualify.

  Note: A co-op (i.e., co-operative) is a legal entity, which is normally a corporation which owns real estate. Equity co-op is a building whereby you buy a share. Collectively all shareholders have the exclusive right to occupy their unit. Another type of co-operative is a non-share capital co-op that has fee-paying members that have the right to occupy a unit. Each province may have different types or definitions of a co-op. Check with your real estate professional or lawyer for clarity on what type qualifies.

Rules can change. Check with CRA for a complete list of the rules and conditions to qualify and how they apply to your individual situation.

2.1 How to withdraw and repay your RRSP funds

It is a reasonably easy process to withdraw your RRSP funds. Start by obtaining a form called T1036 (Home Buyers' Plan [HBP] Request to Withdraw Funds from an RRSP). Your mortgage professional or CRA may provide you with the form. Complete Area 1 of the form then take it to your RRSP issuer to be processed. Some mortgage professionals will assist or even handle this task for you.

You will receive a T4RSP (Statement of Registered Retirement Savings Plan Income) showing the withdrawal. You will be responsible for filing an income tax return beginning the year you make your Home Buyers' Plan (HBP) withdrawal and for each year afterwards until the funds have been repaid.

Remember, you are required to repay what you withdraw over a maximum 15 years in annual repayments of one-fifteenth of whatever you have borrowed. You begin repaying to your RRSP in the second year following the year you made your withdrawal. Each year you will be sent an HBP Statement of Account with your notice of assessment or reassessment. It is wise to keep this statement as it outlines your balance and the amount you have to repay the following year. You simply make contributions to any of your RRSPs in the year repayment is due or in the first 60 days of the following year.

If you wish, you are able to repay more than the required balance for the year. If this is the case, you will reduce the HBP outstanding balance for later years. However, you are still required to make the stated payment for the following year. If you pay less than the required amount, you will have to include the amount not repaid as income on your tax return for that year.

You are allowed to continue contributing to your RRSP. Check with your accounting professional on the specifics regarding proper filing of the repayment form. Remember, if you don't repay the annual amount you owe for that year, the difference will be included in your income and taxed.

There are special rules if circumstances change during the 15-year payback period. For example, if after a qualifying home is bought or built you should move outside the country and become a nonresident, the outstanding amount is repayable within a specific time frame, usually no later than 60 days after you become a nonresident or before the date you file your return for the year. If you do not make the repayment by the deadline, you will have to include the amount that you have not repaid in your income for the year that you became a nonresident. Seek tax advice to ensure you are in compliance with the repayment rules and ensure you know the deadline.

Getting older also means restrictions; at the end of the year that you celebrate your 71st birthday, you are not able to contribute to your RRSPs anymore. You have the option of either contributing all or part of the balance owed in the HBP during this last year. If there is a balance that you still owe, this amount will be added to your income for each year remaining in your repayment time and it will be the amount that you would have been required to pay each year.

In the event of death, the balance at the time of death is included on the deceased's final return. However, if the deceased has a spouse or common-law partner (he or she must be a Canadian resident), the survivor can elect and jointly decide with the deceased's legal representative to make the repayments and not report the balance on a final tax return for the deceased. In essence, the deceased HBP balance becomes the surviving spouse or common-law partner's HBP balance and the survivor makes the repayments to the individual RRSP. Consult with an accountant, a legal professional, or the CRA for clarification of options.

Some exemptions may also exist. It is important that you understand the rules as they apply to your personal situation, and remember, rules can change. It is recommended that you consult either an accountant or a lawyer to ensure you fully understand the rules, qualifications, and obligations. If in doubt ask, and where possible, get it in writing.

Two caveats if you are considering borrowing from your RRSP to purchase a home:

- You will miss many years of tax-sheltered compounding of your retirement funds which were withdrawn, which could make a big difference in the value of your RRSP.

- Some RRSP funds are locked in and are either very expensive or even impossible to withdraw.

3. Moving Expenses

If you move a reasonable distance (as defined by CRA), the federal government allows you to deduct eligible moving expenses. If your move is a minimum of 40 kilometres (by the shortest usual public route) for the reasons of employment, or to study as a student full time at a postsecondary school, or to carry on business, and your new home is your principal residence, you may qualify.

Eligible expenses include transportation and storage costs for household items as well as travel expenses such as meals, accommodations, and vehicle expenses to move you and members of your home to your new place of residence. Consult with a tax professional for advice on this possible deduction.

4. Land Transfer Tax Programs

Ontario, British Columbia, and Prince Edward Island have land transfer tax rebate programs available for home buyers.

4.1 Ontario land transfer tax rebate

When you purchase land or an interest in land in Ontario, you are required to pay on registration of your deed a land transfer tax. Land includes existing buildings, buildings to be constructed, and fixtures. The amount of tax is a mathematical calculation based on the purchase price as follows:

- 0.5 percent on amounts up to and including the first $55,000

- 1 percent of the amount exceeding $55,000 to and including $250,000

- 1.5 percent of the amount exceeding $250,000

- 2 percent of the amount exceeding $400,000 where the land contains one and not more than two single-family residences

If you purchase a home in the city of Toronto, you will pay, in addition to the provincial land transfer tax, another tax called the Municipal Land Transfer Tax (MLTT). The MLTT is charged on a graduated basis similar to the Ontario land transfer tax, for property containing one, and not more than two single-family residences. The MLTT calculation is as follows:

- Up to and including $55,000, the rate is 0.5 percent

- $55,000 to $400,000, the rate is 1 percent

- More than $400,000, the rate is 2 percent

At this time, there is a provincial Land Transfer Tax Refund program available for first-time home buyers. The rules for the program include the following:

- You must be a first-time home buyer, a minimum of 18 years old, and you cannot have owned a home or an interest in a home anywhere in the world.

- If the purchaser has a spouse, the same rules apply for the spouse. If this is the case, no refund is available to either spouse.

  Note: For land transfer tax purposes, a spouse is defined as either of two persons who are married to each other, or are the natural or adoptive parents of a child, or who have cohabited continuously for a period of not less than three years, or in a relationship of some permanence.

- The purchaser must live in the home as his or her principal residence within nine months after the date of transfer of title.

- First-time buyers must apply for a refund within 18 months after the date which the transfer occurred.

Upon registration of your deed or transfer, your lawyer normally completes the appropriate tax statements in the electronic land registration system. If you claim the refund at the time of registration of the transfer of title, you can offset whatever land transfer tax you would normally pay at the time up to a maximum of $2,000. In other words, the refund can be deducted from the land transfer tax that would be due on closing and registration. The maximum amount of the refund is $2,000. Any land transfer tax owed in excess of $2,000 would still be due and payable on registration.

If this refund is not applied for at the time of registration, you will be required to pay the tax; within 18 months after the date of registration you can apply for the refund with the Ministry of Revenue (they will not pay you interest on the refund). You will be required to send the following documentation:

- Ontario Land Transfer Tax Refund Affidavit for First-Time Purchasers of Eligible Homes

- Copy of registered deed, transfer or conveyance, and a copy of docket summary if you registered the transfer electronically. If it wasn't electronically registered, you will need to supply a copy of the Land Registry Office's original which shows the tax paid

- Copy of the agreement of purchase and sale and any schedules and/or amendments attached

- Copy of statement of adjustments

- Proof of the amount of tax that was paid on registration

- Document that proves occupancy of the home such as a copy of telephone or cable bills, driver's licence, or magazine subscription

Additional information or assistance can be obtained from the Ministry of Finance at www.rev.gov.on.ca/en/refund/newhome/index.html.

Note: For first-time home buyers in the city of Toronto, you may also be eligible for a rebate of the MLTT (in addition to the Ontario land transfer tax refund) up to a maximum total of $3,725. This combined maximum total for eligible first-time home buyers is $5,725. Your lawyer may be able to claim the rebate electronically when your transfer or deed is registered. For additional information about the Toronto MLTT rebate contact the call centre at 416-392-4936 or 416-395-6734.

4.2 British Columbia property transfer tax exemption

British Columbia home buyers pay what is called Property Transfer Tax when a transfer is registered. It is a land registration tax and is paid at the Land Title Office to register changes to a certificate of title. The amount of tax is based on the fair market value of the property being transferred, and the calculation is 1 percent on the first $200,000 of the fair market value of the property plus 2 percent on the fair market value of more than $200,000. Fair market value is often the purchase price of the property; however it is defined as the price that a willing buyer and willing seller would pay/receive on the open market.

A gift of property still requires a property transfer tax to be paid. The transaction is taxable at the fair market value of the property regardless of the purchase price.

First-time home buyers may qualify for an exemption from property transfer tax depending on the fair market value of the home. Additional qualifying criteria include the following:

- You must be a first-time buyer. You cannot have owned an interest in a principal residence anywhere in the world at any time.

- You must be a Canadian citizen or permanent Canadian resident and meet the residency requirement of having lived in British Columbia for 12 consecutive months immediately prior to the date of registration of transfer of the property. If this is not the case, you may be eligible if you have filed two income tax returns as a British Columbia resident during the six years prior to the date you register the property.

- You cannot have ever received a first-time buyer's home refund or exemption.

- You cannot exceed the fair market value threshold for eligible residential property of $425,000 (only if purchasing an existing home). Proportional exemptions may exist for eligible residences with a fair market value of up to $450,000 (check the eligibility requirements).

- The land must be 0.5 hectares (1.24 acres) or smaller.

- The property will only be used as your principal residence.

You might qualify for a partial exemption if the property does not meet all of the requirements.

Normally, your lawyer or a notary applies for your exemption when the property is registered. The Land Title Office (or equivalent in your area) will send your application to the Ministry to verify your eligibility. You may apply for a refund within 18 months from the date of the original transfer or registration of title if you don't apply when the transfer is registered.

You will need to occupy the property within 92 days of registration. The property must be used as your principal residence for the remainder of the first year after you register the property. You may retain a partial exemption if you move before the end of the first year. A principal residence needs to be built on vacant land within one year of the date of registration of the land and you will need to occupy the property for the remainder of the year. The fair market value of the land as of the date of registration plus the cost to build the home cannot be greater than $450,000.

Additional information is available from the Ministry of Finance at www.sbr.gov.bc.ca (accessed November, 2011).

4.3 Prince Edward Island first-time buyer land transfer tax rebate

In Prince Edward Island the land transfer tax is calculated as 1 percent of purchase price or assessed value of the property, whichever is greater.

There is no transfer tax on property value or assessed value of less than $30,000.

First-time home buyers are exempt from paying land transfer tax if the property value or assessed value (whichever is greater) is not more than $200,000, and the home will be occupied as a primary residence.

If the first-time buyer wants to apply for the real property tax exemption, he or she must complete a Declaration — First-time Home Buyers form, which needs to be signed by a notary public or commissioner. The first-time buyer must also sign an oath stating that he or she is a Canadian citizen or permanent resident, has met a residency requirement in the province, is at least 18 years of age or older, has not owned a principal residence home previously, and has not previously obtained a first-time home buyer's exemption.

For additional information, go to www.taxandland.pe.ca.

5. First-Time Home Buyers' Tax Credit (HBTC)

The federal government introduced, in 2009, a non-refundable tax credit which is based on the amount of $5,000 for certain home buyers that purchase a *qualifying* home. The credit is calculated by multiplying the lowest personal income tax rate for the year by $5,000 (15 percent in 2009). In 2009, the credit was $750. A buyer claims the first-time Home Buyers' Tax Credit (HBTC) in the taxation year in which the qualifying home was acquired.

To be eligible, you or your spouse or common-law partner must have bought a qualifying home; and you cannot have lived in another home owned by your spouse or common-law partner in the year of purchase or in any of the four preceding years.

The home must be in Canada, and can be an existing home or one under construction. Single family; semidetached; condominium units; townhouses; apartments in duplexes, triplexes, fourplexes, and apartment buildings; as well as mobile homes qualify. A share in a co-operative housing corporation that entitles you to possess and gives you equity interest in a housing unit qualifies. A share of a co-operative that only provides tenancy does not qualify.

If you are disabled or are purchasing a home for a related person with a disability, you don't have to be a first-time home buyer in this case. The home must be acquired to enable the person with the disability to live in a more accessible dwelling. However, you must intend to occupy the home or must intend that the related person with a disability will occupy the home as a principal residence not later than a year after it is acquired.

The HBTC is a separate plan from the Home Buyers' Plan (HBP) and you can participate in both.

For additional information visit www.cra-arc.gc.ca/hbtc. Speak to your accountant for specific filing details and forms.

Programs can be confusing and rules can change. It is recommended that you review the rules and conditions with your legal and accounting professionals prior to committing to a home purchase, to determine whether you qualify for any or all of the home-buyers' programs.

It is imperative that you understand how the programs work and relate to your personal circumstances. It really pays to get expert advice prior to making any home-buying decision or signing any contracts.

6. Green Home Program

Not only will you save energy by buying an energy-efficient home or making energy-efficient renovations to a home, you may be eligible to receive a 10 percent refund on your Canada Mortgage and Housing Corporation (CMHC) mortgage loan insurance premium, along with an extended amortization up to a maximum of 30 years, without a surcharge for a high-ratio mortgage.

You will need to find out if the home you are considering buying meets one of the following requirements:

- The home was built or will be built under a CMHC-eligible energy-efficient building program.

- The home is an energy-efficient R-2000 model.

- A qualified Natural Resources Canada (NRCan) advisor has assessed the home and the home has an energy rating of a minimum of 80.

- The unit you are buying is located in a building that is 25 percent more energy efficient than if constructed, meeting the requirements of the Model National Energy Code for Buildings (MNECB) (only for condominiums).

You can find out the home's energy rating by having an energy-efficiency assessment by an NRCan advisor, obtaining an R-2000 certificate (where applicable), or having your builder provide a declaration from CMHC that the builder is a member of the CMHC energy-efficient building program. For condominiums, obtain a letter from NRCan.

If you plan to build a new home and it is not an R-2000 builder, you can also have an energy advisor evaluate the builder to ensure the home meets CMHC's requirements.

To be eligible for the refund, if the home you are planning to buy has an energy rating of less than 80, you will need to obtain the energy assessment from an NRCan qualified energy advisor and then renovate your home using part of the CMHC insured funds based on the recommendations provided by the assessor, to increase your energy score by at least 5 points to a minimum of 40.

The assessor will need to conduct a second assessment once the renovations are completed to confirm that the energy rating has increased by at least 5 points and is at a minimum overall rating of 40.

Contact CMHC or your mortgage professional for additional information on the Green Home program.

7. New Immigrant and Self-Employed Program

As a newcomer to Canada, or a self-employed home buyer, acquiring a mortgage can be a different process than that of a traditional borrower with an established credit rating and a history of employment with a firm. Lenders offer different mortgage products for the new immigrant and self-employed borrower.

Understandably, new immigrant applicants often do not have an established credit history in Canada. For those that don't have a Canadian credit score, a satisfactory international credit bureau or a satisfactory letter of reference from a bank in their country of origin, along with evidence that they have liquid assets available that are equal to at least six months of principal, interest, and taxes in addition to current confirmation of the required down payment may be acceptable to some lenders. Normally, the borrower must be a resident of Canada with landed immigrant status or confirm that an application for landed immigrant status has been made, received, and acknowledged by Citizenship and Immigration Canada.

Lenders may, depending on the borrower, agree to finance an insured mortgage up to 95 percent of the appraised value of a home. To qualify, lenders usually ask the borrower for a variety of different documentation along with confirmation of income and down payment. Of course, lenders usually want to see a good credit score as well. Depending on the value of the loan, and the lender, often to qualify you will need to have landed immigrant status. Normally the lender will review and assess your overall situation such as your net worth, your employment history, saving habits, and credit score.

Terms and conditions of the mortgages offered can vary depending on the strength of the borrower; however, maximum amortizations range from 25 to 30 years and fixed-rate, short-term, long-term, variable rate, and open or closed mortgages are usually available.

CMHC as well as Genworth Financial Canada offer mortgage default insurance programs, insuring up to 95 percent of the appraised value of the home for new immigrants, with up to a 30-year maximum amortization period. The borrower will also need to qualify based on the insurer's criteria and will be required to pay the mortgage default insurance premium where applicable.

Self-employed borrowers are usually asked to supply income tax notices of assessment or reassessment for the last two years along with confirmation that no outstanding income tax is owed. Applicants who are unable to provide standard confirmation of declared income will usually need to meet a minimum credit score depending on the loan-to-value ratio of the mortgage. Maximum loan-to-value varies depending on the strength of the borrower; mortgage default insurance criteria as well as lender underwriting guidelines may be different for self-employed borrowers. Mortgage default insurance premiums can be higher for self-employed borrowers. Speak with your lender or check with CMHC or Genworth Financial Canada regarding premiums.

Although lenders have guidelines that they must adhere to, each borrower is assessed separately taking into account several factors. Sometimes adding a co-borrower or a non-occupant guarantor can further strengthen an application.

The mortgage industry is competitive, rules and programs change, and mortgage professionals want good quality customers. Fortunately, many lenders understand the value of new immigrants and self-employed borrowers. Discuss options and any guidelines with a mortgage professional.

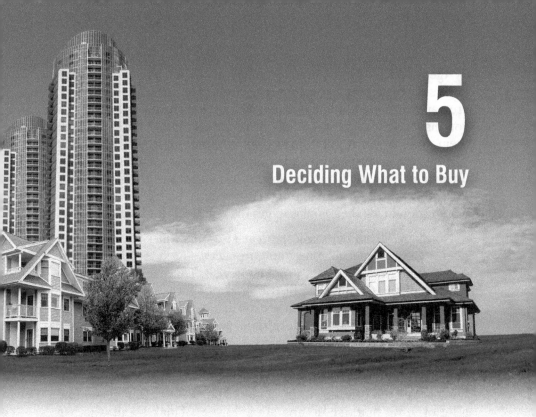

5

Deciding What to Buy

There are pros and cons for both new homes and resale homes. New homes are functionally up to date, usually more energy efficient, and they are "new" so you can begin with a clean slate. However, on the flip side, you may be spending additional money for appliances, upgrades, decks, window treatments, landscaping, fencing, and decorating.

Existing or resale homes are already built, so you see exactly what you get. You can walk through the home, see how it feels, evaluate the size of the rooms, and check the overall flow of the floor plan. Depending on the age of the home, the neighbourhood may be established and built up, and the community amenities and facilities such as schools, shopping, recreation, and transportation may already be in place. Backyards may be fenced and landscaping mature. On the negative side, depending on the age of the property, the home could be dated, functionally obsolete, or require updates.

1. Buying a Newly Built Home

Newly built homes are often marketed and sold through the builders' site offices which are staffed by the builders' salespeople. In some cases, the builders' salespeople are licensed real estate professionals, but in other cases they are not.

Agency disclosure requirements may vary depending on provincial laws and whether the salespeople are licensed or not. The salespeople are happy to show you the builder's homes and answer any questions you may have, but be careful about how much information you give them. You should not tell them your motivation for wanting to buy (e.g., you need to move by a certain date) or personal financial information. You don't want to appear too anxious as this could have a negative effect on you getting a better deal. Builders' salespeople work for builders; their goal is to get the best deals for builders.

Normally, a builder's salesperson at a site will show you floor plans, features, specifications, and upgrades. Often there are model homes built (and decorated) for you to visit. This enables you to get an idea of the layout, size, distribution of space, and possible upgrades and enhancements that are available. Be careful; often these model homes are upgraded, furnished, and decorated, which creates an emotional bond to the property; it may even entice you to purchase one of the homes. Upgrades and extras usually cost additional money, sometimes substantially more money than the base model. Understand this prior to visiting a model home. Often builders make a lot of profit marking up upgraded finishes. Think about whether the cost of the upgrades will bring you additional resale value, or if you are better off completing the upgrades after closing.

The great thing about buying a newly constructed home is that everything is new! The appliances, operating systems, flooring, and cabinets will all be new and ready for you to use! You don't have to redecorate or clean! Normally, you will also be able to choose the finishes, colours, materials, and upgrades that you like. However, be aware, upgrades may be at an additional cost. Make sure you ask what is included and what may be offered at an extra cost.

1.1 Functionally modern layout, features, and current technology

New homes are designed and built with current consumer wants and industry trends in mind. Homes built several years ago can be *functionally obsolete* meaning they do not reflect today's consumer wants and needs in terms of layout and features (e.g., large eat-in kitchens, large closets). Today there is more of a focus on family rooms or great rooms and less on formal living and dining rooms. Current new homes in general offer larger and lavish en suite baths as well as additional storage options. Sometimes you may have the opportunity to remove or move and modify walls, add upgrades, and change flooring to customize the new home to your individual wants and needs.

New homes are usually technologically advanced, offering energy-efficient devices and ventilation systems. Some even come with high-speed Internet and security systems already set up that may be compatible with technological devices such as iPods and home-theatre systems. These are considered *smart homes*.

Over time building codes are updated, and the latest advances in materials, maintenance-free finishes, and equipment are used to build new homes. Research builders. Consider visiting new homes or condominiums built by the same builder and talk with owners; ask about after-closing services and if deficiencies noted in the pre-delivery inspection were corrected.

1.2 Green standards

There are builders that create or customize homes to fit current green standards using materials with fewer chemicals. Some homes are built to minimize maintenance as they are made of materials that do not need painting (e.g., vinyl siding on windows and doors instead of wood).

Canada Mortgage and Housing Corporation (CMHC) offers a mortgage loan insurance premium refund when you purchase an energy-efficient home (or when you make energy-saving renovations). You could also have the flexibility of extending the amortization up to a maximum of 30 years without a premium surcharge. Check with CMHC on requirements to obtain a refund. See Chapter 4 for more information.

1.3 New home warranties

New homes often come with a warranty. The coverage varies depending on the province and the warranty provider. In BC, Ontario, and Québec, third-party warranties are mandatory; in other provinces these are optional. Be careful in provinces in which warranties are not mandatory because some lenders will not give mortgages unless you have a warranty. To get third-party warranty coverage you have to purchase a home from a builder who participates in and registers your home with the warranty program. Check with the warranty provider for a list of builder members.

When you are deciding on a new home builder, one of the important items to consider is warranty; find out what is covered and for how long. Warranties usually cover defects in structure, workmanship, and materials or parts. Usually just prior to closing on a new purchase you will do a Pre-Delivery Inspection (PDI) with a builder representative. During this inspection you will walk through the property and examine the builder's work, noting anything that looks incomplete, missing, or deficient. A report is filled out noting these items, and the builder is obligated to fix them — usually within the first year.

Warranty coverage and programs vary depending on the region in which you are purchasing your home. Alberta, Saskatchewan, and Manitoba have a variety of providers and warranty programs with most offering deposit protection and one-year protection for defects in materials and work.

Five-year structural defect coverage up to certain maximum limitations may also be available. For more information go to the National Home Warranty program's website (www.nationalhomewarranty. com). The following sections discuss provincial warranty programs.

Programs, rules, conditions, and laws change. This is an example of the types of coverage that may be available. For additional information about new home warranties check with the warranty provider in the province you choose to buy or build a new home.

1.3a Ontario's Tarion Warranty Corporation

Tarion Warranty Corporation is an independent not-for-profit corporation that provides warranties on newly built homes in Ontario. Tarion administers the *Ontario New Home Warranties Plan Act*; the Act states that new home and condominium builders must provide warranty protection to their customers.

Coverage includes deposit protection, protection against defects in work and materials, delayed closings or occupancies without proper notice, and protection against unauthorized substitutions. There is a one-year, two-year, and seven-year warranty protection against major structural defects. There are specific rules for warranty coverage for registered condominium corporations and their common elements; check with Tarion for more details.

The aggregate maximum warranty coverage under the one-year, two-year, and major structural defect warranties is $300,000. Tarion protects up to a maximum of $40,000 of your deposit on new houses, and up to a maximum of $20,000 on new condominiums. Payments made for upgrades and extras may not be protected. You need to have a signed agreement of purchase and sale in order to qualify for coverage.

For additional information and details on what is included and excluded, and how to make a claim, go to www.tarion.com.

1.3b British Columbia New Home Warranty

Warranty coverage is mandatory in British Columbia. The coverage includes two years of protection on labour and materials (some limits apply), five years on the building envelope, which includes water penetration, and ten years on major structural defects.

It is prudent for home buyers to verify that the builder is licensed, which you can do by going to the website of the Public Registry of Residential Builders (www.hpo.bc.ca/public-registry-residential-builders). Note that home warranty insurance can only be provided by insurance companies that are approved by the provincial Financial Institutions Commission (www.fic.gov.bc.ca).

1.3c Alberta New Home Warranty Program

Alberta's new home warranty coverage (for single-family dwellings) includes protection for up to $100,000 to repair defects in workmanship and materials during the first year after possession. The unused portion of the first year materials and workmanship warranty coverage amount up to $100,000 can be applied to costs to repair major structural defects affecting the load bearing components in the first five years. You may also decide to purchase an extended Structural Integrity Warranty Protection for an additional five years, which gives you a total of ten years of structural protection.

Single-family dwellings are covered for up to $50,000 including $3,000 in legal fees towards the completion costs of discharge of builders' liens should the home not be completed as contracted.

Deposit protection up to 20 percent of the purchase price to a maximum of $100,000 is covered if the builder defaults. Condominium deposit coverage is up to 15 percent of the purchase price to a maximum of $30,000, whichever is less.

Multi-family home coverage is available for up to $60,000 per unit in costs to repairs defects in workmanship and materials during the first year after possession, subject to the lesser of $60,000 per unit or $1,500,000 total for the project. The coverage amount not used to repair workmanship or deficiencies can also be applied to costs to repair major structural defects affecting load-bearing components of the unit in the first five years, which is subject to maximums.

For additional information visit the Alberta New Home Warranty Program (www.anhwp.com).

1.3d Québec

Since 1999, new residential dwellings have been covered by a mandatory guarantee plan. As the private administrator, La Garantie des maisons neuves (GMN) de l'Association provinciale des constructeurs d'habitations du Québec (APCHQ), the Québec builders association new-home warranty program acts as guarantor for certain contractual obligations of the builder.

For additional information on what is covered and excluded and the maximum amounts, as well as information on the type of buildings covered, refer to the Association de la construction du Québec (www.acq.org).

1.3e Atlantic Home Warranty

Atlantic Home Warranty (AHW) is a seven-year limited warranty that includes one-year protection against defects in materials supplied by the builder. It also includes optional deposit protection up to a maximum of $20,000 and protection against major structural defects. Check the fine print to determine coverage, maximum limits, and times. For more information go to AHW's website (www.ahwp.org).

1.4 Long closing

Buying a brand new home often comes with a long closing — sometimes 12 to 24 months — which allows you to purchase at today's prices. This of course helps in a rising market as it insulates you against an increase in price. As an incentive, some builders allow buyers to hold a property with a minimal down payment (e.g., $1,000 to $2,000 down payment) and offer graduated deposits over time. This enables first-time buyers to accumulate their down payment while the home is being built.

Some builders offer to lock in the interest rate for this length of time, which helps the first-time buyer against potential future rate increases. Make sure that you read the fine print regarding builder mortgages, especially if a lower-than-market interest rate is offered.

Additionally, sometimes new home builders offer financing assistance as an incentive (and convenience) for buyers to purchase one of their homes or condominiums. See Chapter 2, section **1.5** for more about builders' mortgages.

1.5 Harmonized Sales Tax (HST) and Goods and Services Tax (GST)

The Harmonized Sales Tax (HST) or Goods and Services Tax (GST) is included in the purchase price. The type of tax you pay depends on where you purchase. Alberta, Northwest Territories, Yukon, and Nunavut do not have provincial or territorial sales tax. Canada Revenue Agency (CRA) has a GST or HST new home rebate program that provides a rebate on part of the GST or HST paid on the purchase or construction of most new homes that are being used as a principal residence. The GST and the federal part of the HST may be reduced from 5 percent to approximately 3.5 percent for homes valued at $350,000 or less. Homes valued between $350,000 to a maximum of $450,000 may be eligible to receive a lesser rebate. HST/GST rules are complicated and vary. Get legal advice prior to purchasing your home. Contact CRA for additional information.

1.6 New home builder's agreement of purchase and sale

The builder's agreement of purchase and sale is usually lengthy and cumbersome, and the terms, conditions, and clauses are worded to the benefit of the builder/seller. There is no "standard" new-home contract as each is individually drafted by a lawyer who represents the builder. It is very important that you seek legal counsel prior to signing a new-home agreement of purchase and sale, especially if you don't understand the legal terms contained in the agreement. The lawyer will not advise you on whether he or she thinks you're getting a good deal, only on the legalese in the contract. It is recommended that prior to signing any builder contract that you and your lawyer review the contract to ensure that you are familiar and comfortable with all the clauses and costs.

Generally, the builder's agreement of purchase and sale describes the finished home in detail including but not limited to material type, finishes, construction specifics, grading, and landscaping. The agreement of purchase and sale will outline planned closing dates as well as notices, costs, responsibilities for delays, warranties, predelivery inspections, anticipated extra closing costs, and builder and home buyer responsibilities. Any upgrades or extras you may want will be contained in a schedule, which outlines the costs and details.

Often your lawyer will recommend changes and deletions to the builder contract prior to you proceeding. Depending on the builder and what the requested changes are, sometimes the builder will be accommodating, but every situation is different.

If the home is not yet built, the builder will include specific clauses related to the building and completion of the home. One of the most important clauses for the buyer of a new home is the closing date. The closing date may not be confirmed (only estimated) and the closing date may be extended. As the home may not be built when you agree to buy it, numerous things can occur such as contractors going on strike, delays in obtaining building permits, or material shortages.

Builders normally have extension provisions built into the agreement of purchase and sale. This makes planning your move tricky. It is important that you understand the extension notice time frames. In some cases you may even be eligible for financial compensation or the right to void the transaction if problems fall outside the stated notices.

Details regarding the building of the home will be included. You may find clauses that allow the builder to make substitutions for materials or to reverse layouts — often without you being notified. Understand your rights and options in advance; otherwise, you may be surprised and disappointed.

There will likely be a section regarding home warranty so that you understand exactly what is covered and for how long. With respect to the warranty, determine if there is deposit protection and for what amount. What happens if the builder goes bankrupt and you have paid a deposit? Depending on your coverage and the province where you purchase, you may be eligible to be reimbursed or partially reimbursed from a warranty program. Any deposit in excess of the deposit protection will not be covered.

Depending on the province, there may be a municipality levy to cover the cost of roads, schools, and other facilities. In Ontario (and perhaps other provinces) sometimes there is even a subdivision damage or grading deposit that may be refundable to you after a period of time, but only if you ask for it back. You may have to wait a year or two to apply for it. These expenses are often already built into the purchase price.

There may be a new-home warranty clause making you responsible for payment of this warranty. This is especially important in areas where new-home warranties are mandatory.

If you are arranging for a mortgage, determine in advance if there is a mortgage rate lock-in or guarantee and for how long. Also, what occurs should the closing be delayed with the rate lock-in — is it also extended?

When purchasing a freehold property (as opposed to a condominium) ask if the lot is registered, and if not, what the estimated time is for this to occur. A builder may not be able to obtain building permits if the lot is not registered. Speak with a legal professional about this and your options.

In Ontario, new condo developers are required to give you a disclosure statement which includes copies of the first year's proposed budget, declaration, and description. You have a ten-day cooling off period during which you can change your mind, cancel, and receive a refund of your deposit. This cooling-off is not available to buyers of new houses.

Ask the builder for a breakdown of any other expenses (e.g., utility hookups, warranty premium, upgrades) in addition to the purchase price of the home. You may be able to add a clause that puts a cap on all extra charges so you know the maximum you will have to pay on closing. The new home builder's agreement of purchase and sale is a complex document that may contain numerous clauses and schedules, which can be overwhelming for the new home buyer to understand. These are examples of items that may be in a builder's agreement; there will be additional terms and conditions. Processes, clauses, expenses, and laws vary depending on the province. Always seek independent legal advice.

2. Buying a Resale Home

While a new home offers many benefits and is right for some home buyers, often a new home buyer purchases a home from plans, photos, and drawings which is possibly all they see prior to making the buying commitment. With respect to a resale home, it is already built so you see exactly what it looks like. You are usually able to walk through and inspect the home.

Often, with a resale home, you will also get upgrades and extras included such as finished basement, appliances, fencing, landscaping, window coverings, upgraded electric light fixtures, and decorating. This is an advantage to you when the home is well cared for and the upgrades and extras suit your tastes.

A nice thing about buying a resale home is that you will be able to see your potential new neighbourhood. Compared to new homes, it is easier to learn about a neighbourhood because people are already living there. It is a good idea to walk and drive through neighbourhoods and talk to residents. Stand back and look at the streets; are the lawns well-manicured? What about traffic noises, or other developments? You get to view the neighbourhood; depending on the age of the neighbourhood, you may see parks, schools, places of worship, shopping, medical facilities, recreational and other facilities.

Another bonus to buying a resale home in an established neighbourhood is that there will be less construction in the immediate area. You won't be living with mud, dirt, and noisy construction. In established neighbourhoods you will find that trees are grown and developed as are landscaping, gardens, parks, and amenities; in a newly developed area these things may not exist yet.

There will also be services and facilities that have been developed and are in operation. You can visit schools, shopping centres, churches, and recreational areas if they are important to you.

Any builder defects or issues (e.g., settlement, nail pops) that came up in the first year or two have likely been fixed in a resale home. Additionally, with a resale home, you may get upgrades included that do not represent the full value of what it costs to add them. For example, an in-ground swimming pool may have originally cost $35,000 to build; however, you may have only paid a few thousand dollars for this improvement compared to a similar market-value home on the street without a pool. Some upgrades are only worth a fraction of their original cost on the resale market.

2.1 Home warranty on a resale home

You can purchase a home warranty on a resale home. There are several providers of home warranty coverage for resale properties and the costs are quite reasonable. Normally resale warranties cover heating, air conditioning, plumbing, duct work, ventilation, sump pumps, and wells. Deductibles apply and vary with the provider and coverage offered.

Read the fine print on warranties because they may not cover structural defects such as a leaky roof or basement. Your insurance broker may be able to suggest a few insurers to speak with about this coverage.

2.2 The resale agreement of purchase and sale contract

The resale agreement of purchase and sale is usually a lot simpler and shorter than a new home agreement. It is typically a pre-printed standard form with schedules attached to allow the addition of clauses relevant to the transaction. These standard forms are issued either by the province or local real estate board.

Aside from the obvious (e.g., property address, buyer and seller names, price, deposit, closing, included and excluded chattels and fixtures), there will be other terms in the agreement of purchase and sale such as clauses related to title, title search, warranties, residency, subdivision and planning act — all of which your lawyer will review with you. If you wish to add contingencies (conditions to protect yourself) such as finance, home inspection, insurance confirmation, or insurance conditions, these clauses are normally added on a separate schedule.

Although the resale agreement of purchase and sale agreement is simpler than the new home agreement, it is still recommended that you have a lawyer review it (prior to signing it), to ensure that you understand and are accepting of the legal provisions within the contract. This is likely your single largest investment so be cautious and understand all the terms, conditions, and responsibilities. You don't want any unwanted surprises.

3. Freeholds and Condominiums

Now that you have an overview of some of the differences between buying a new home and a resale property, you will need to decide whether you prefer a freehold or condominium property. (**Note:** In BC the term *strata* is often used interchangeably with condominium.)

Condominium and freehold are types of ownership. A condominium homeowner owns a specific unit, and a percentage interest in common areas (e.g., hallways, lobby, elevator, outside grounds, recreation facilities) which are shared with other owners. Sometimes unit owners have the *exclusive use* of facilities such as backyards of townhouses, parking, and lockers. It is important to know and understand exactly what you own and what you have exclusive use of — this can vary depending on the condominium property and province. Condominiums in Ontario have a Declaration and Description document. The declaration contains rights of ownership, restrictions, and obligations.

Freehold ownership means that you own the property within pre-set lot lines, along with the actual dwelling. You are responsible for the maintenance and care of the driveway, exterior, and land, as well as the interior. There normally is no monthly maintenance fee. When buyers think of freehold property they are usually referring to detached, link, semidetached, and possibly townhouses.

Provincial or territorial condominium legislation and guidelines regulate how condominiums are created. It is recommended that you find out who is managing the condominium corporation and what the track record is.

Look around at the overall appearance of the common areas because this will give you an overview of how well the property is managed. Typically with condominium ownership, the owner of a unit pays a share (usually each month) for the management and maintenance of the common areas. The condominium corporation calculates how owners pay shares based on interest owned in common elements and other factors. In Ontario, a part of this monthly fee is allocated or held in a *reserve* fund to pay for major updates and repairs such as roofs, plumbing, and parking garages. Check the laws in your province.

Prior to committing to purchasing a condominium unit, it is important and prudent to refer to the financial statements of a condominium corporation to determine whether the condominium is in good financial health and what the planned future expenditures will be and at what estimated cost. This is especially important if you are considering purchasing a unit in an older condominium property as you want to confirm there is enough money in the reserve fund to pay for the anticipated or projected repairs. If there is a deficiency, then the condominium unit owners could be forced to pay a special assessment, which might result in you paying literally thousands of dollars. Some buyers include a condition on a satisfactory home inspection by a qualified home inspector, especially if the Declaration or equivalent indicates you are responsible for maintenance and repair of systems such as heating, air conditioning, plumbing and the like.

Condominium properties have bylaws and rules. Each province may have different, specific laws that govern these areas; seek legal advice. It is wise to be aware of the bylaws and rules prior to committing to purchasing a condominium unit. Ask the seller, developer, broker, or the condominium management company for a copy of the budget along with the bylaws and rules in advance. In Ontario, this is usually contained in the condominium's "status certificate."

Also included in the status certificate is the Declaration, description, bylaws and rules, copy of any reserve fund study, and information about lawsuits or special assessments. Buyers often have their lawyers review the status certificate and related documents beforehand or as a condition of purchasing the condominium unit to ensure that the reserve fund is large enough to cover anticipated repairs or renovations, and to ensure there are no special assessments or pending legal actions against or by the condominium corporation.

Condominium ownership is available with most building structures including apartments, townhomes, single detached, semidetached homes, and duplexes. Think of it as collective or shared ownership. When you are inspecting existing condominium structures, especially if they are apartment-type structures, inquire about the following:

- **How secure is the building?** For example, does it have security cameras and where are they located? Is security manned by a person or is it an electronic system? Are you notified of guests? How easy is it for visitors to bypass security?

- **Is there parking?** Do you own a parking space or more than one parking space? Is there guest parking and what is the availability for it?

- **What type of insurance will you need to purchase?** You will probably need to obtain contents, liability, and possibly internal structural insurance (e.g., for kitchen cabinets, bathroom fixtures, wiring, plumbing). Find out what the condominium corporation's master policy covers and whether or not it is limited to the common areas.

- **What type of recreation facilities are included?** Some places include a pool, gym, or tennis court. Is use covered in the purchase price and who has access to the facilities?

While inspecting the condominium unit, listen to hear if the soundproofing between units is adequate. You don't want to hear everything your neighbour does on a daily basis! Additionally, find out about traffic patterns. For example, how close is the unit to noisy areas such as garbage chutes and elevators?

With respect to condominium apartments, usually units on higher floors, especially those with preferred views, cost more to purchase.

Ask if each unit is individually metered for electricity and water. Find out what is included with the monthly maintenance fee. Find out who is responsible for any interior mechanical or operating systems (e.g., plumbing, air conditioning, heating) as well as if management approval is required for any improvements (e.g., replacing broadloom carpets with hardwood flooring) and what the process is to obtain approval.

Most new condominium projects include provisos for graduated deposits over time with the final balance of the purchase price due on the closing date. Keep in mind that most provinces have new home warranties that cover deposit insurance up to a certain maximum amount. If the deposit amount on your purchase exceeds what is covered by the new home warranty coverage, you will be uninsured for the excess amount.

It is wise to find out the rules for leasing your unit. If you decide you eventually want to move to a bigger or different home but keep your condo to rent out, you will need to know if the condominium corporation must first approve the tenant and if there are any restrictions. Laws vary depending on the province and property.

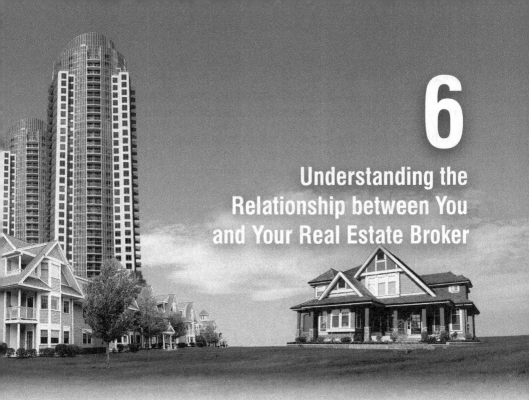

6

Understanding the Relationship between You and Your Real Estate Broker

Many buyers utilize the services of a real estate professional, also called a broker or agent. For simplicity, the terms *broker* and *agent* refer to a real estate professional throughout this chapter except where noted. Your broker can assist you in locating a property, but he or she can also do so much more. This chapter will help you understand the role of your real estate professional, should you choose to work with one.

1. Understanding What Your Real Estate Agent Does

Real estate professionals undergo lengthy schooling to obtain licensing to work in real estate. Upon passing a series of exams, they normally join a local real estate board as well as national and provincial associations. REALTOR® is used to describe a licensed real estate broker or sales representative who is a member of the Canadian Real Estate Association and must subscribe to the Realtor Code of Ethics which contains articles and standards of practice that are strictly enforced.

You may wonder if you need or want a broker to assist you with your home search. Or can you search for a home on your own? Brokers who are members of a real estate board have access to the proprietary Multiple Listing Service® System (see Chapter 7). While members of the public can search and list homes themselves, access to information is limited compared to the professionals' system.

While the Internet has a variety of other public sites that enable you to search for homes, the reality is the information that a broker has is more extensive and updated frequently.

1.1 Tasks of a real estate broker

The role of a real estate broker is not limited to supplying information about which homes are available; brokers play an essential role in your transaction as they can provide you with guidance and assistance in several different areas.

1.1a Determining your plan

During your first meeting with a broker, you will review your "wish list." This will include the ideal areas you would like to live, the types of homes that interest you, and any special or desired features for your home.

1.1b Financing plan

Many brokers will suggest that you meet with a mortgage broker or bank mortgage representative so that you can complete a mortgage application, and discuss and set up a pre-approved mortgage. This is an important part of the home-buying process and should be done at the beginning.

1.1c Researching properties to view

After discussing and reviewing your wants and needs (i.e., buyer profile), the broker will search for available properties that meet your needs, budget, and geographic preferences. An experienced broker will have knowledge of market values and inventory available in your price range.

Normally a broker will begin by searching the local Multiple Listing Service® System of the real estate board for listed homes that meet your criteria, budget, and geographic preferences. He or she will also check for exclusively listed homes. Your broker will extract the homes that best suit your needs and begin educating you on your options and the marketplace. (Processes may vary depending on the province and the agreement you have with the broker.)

1.1d Booking showing appointments

The broker will arrange showing or viewing appointments so that you can walk through the selected properties. It is important to give feedback to your broker on the homes you view so that any modification in the choice of types or areas of homes being selected and shown are appropriate.

1.1e Discussing the viewed homes

Depending on whether you are working with a buyer's agent (the broker who represents you) or not, this discussion could vary. A buyer's agent will provide you with data on the value of homes similar to the ones you are viewing in the general area (this is known as a comparative market analysis).

Examples of other important factors that would also be discussed with a buyer's agent include:

- **Sales trends:** Data supporting an increasing, decreasing, or flat sales trend.

- **Listing to sales ratios:** Number of homes that sell versus the number coming onto the market during the same time frame.

- **Time on market:** How quickly on average homes are selling.

- **Probable future resale:** Demand for the home and area.

1.1f Completing the agreement of purchase and sale

The broker normally completes a "resale" agreement of purchase and sale. A buyer's agent may insert special terms and conditions (clauses) into your agreement that are for your protection. Depending on your situation, conditional clauses may be recommended by your agent such as financing, home inspection, status certificates for condominiums (where appropriate), insurance confirmation, and possibly water or well tests, and septic tests (for rural properties). A buyer's agent will explain and discuss in detail the clauses in your offer.

It is always recommended that you have a lawyer review the agreement of purchase and sale prior to you signing. This recommendation is for your legal protection.

1.1g Connecting you to other relevant professionals

Brokers work with a host of professionals in their day-to-day business. Some of these professionals include mortgage professionals, home inspectors, lawyers, and accountants. You can ask your broker for a list of names of professionals that other clients have had good results with if you wish. It is a good practice to verify references.

1.2 How to find a real estate broker

Finding a real estate broker is an important task. Buying a home is likely your largest single investment and you will be spending a good deal of time with your chosen broker. You should choose a broker with whom you feel comfortable. Ideally, you want a broker who listens, asks questions, and is genuinely interested in assisting you with your purchase. It really does pay to spend sufficient time meeting and interviewing a few brokers.

A referral of a real estate broker by a family member or friend is a good place to start if he or she has had a positive experience. The referred broker should be knowledgeable about the area and property type that you are considering purchasing.

Some brokers work in teams, where there is a lead real estate broker and a group of other real estate professionals who work on the team. Often the various team members specialize in different areas and product types. You want to make sure you understand who will be working directly with you as this is who you will likely spend the majority of your time with; you want to ensure you feel comfortable with this person.

If you have not been referred to a broker, you might want to leaf through the local newspaper and pick the names of a couple of brokers who specialize in and advertise properties for sale in your area of choice and price range. Of course, the sellers are usually being represented by the broker on the advertised properties; however, this will at least provide you with names to begin the interview process.

1.2a Interviewing real estate brokers

It is a good idea to interview a couple of real estate brokers to make a comparison of the services they provide and see how and if they will represent you on your search and buying process.

Ask how well the broker knows the area and type of home you are seeking. Experience is important; so is knowledge and personality. Ask the broker how he or she will inform you about properties and what his or her process is to source and show you homes.

Ask if the broker has any programs that offer special discounts or other options with respect to mortgage financing, movers, and home inspectors. It's also a good idea to meet everyone you will be dealing with during the home-buying process if there will be a team working for you.

At some point during the meeting, give the broker the opportunity to explain how he or she will help you buy your first home. The broker will likely share with you his or her buyer's program (assuming he or she has one). Normally, he or she will also speak about himself or herself, his or her accomplishments, and how he or she will fulfill the role as your real estate broker. From this interview you should get a good sense about the person, his or her practices, and how comfortable you feel with him or her. You may even ask the broker for references from buyers he or she has worked with previously.

Find out if the broker will be representing you as a client or as a customer (see section **2.**). This is very important, especially if you wish for representation in the home-buying process. Ask to see a copy of the written agreement of buyer representation.

2. Who Is Working for You?

The *client* is a consumer who engages a real estate brokerage company to represent him or her in the purchase or sale of real estate. When a buyer is being represented by a brokerage, all the salespeople with the brokerage owe the buyer fiduciary duties that include confidentiality, loyalty, full disclosure, and competence. Normally, this relationship is spelled out in written form in a document called a Buyer Representation Agreement (or a Listing Agreement if you are selling a home).

The *customer* is a consumer who is not being represented by a brokerage company. Although the broker is not providing *representation* services to the customer, he or she must still treat the customer fairly and honestly.

It is important that you understand who the broker is working for — this is known as an agency relationship. The buyer and the seller of a property may have their own agents, meaning they will both have a real estate broker representing them. However, this may not always be the case.

REALTORS®, under their code of ethics, must disclose in writing the nature of the services they are providing, and they should obtain written acknowledgement of the disclosure. They are required to give written representation and customer service agreements to sellers and buyers. You will be asked to sign forms stating that you understand the services provided by the sales representative.

In Ontario, a sales representative and broker are both licensed to trade in real estate. A broker is a licensee that has taken additional courses and passed the corresponding exams. Each real estate brokerage company must have a broker of record. Brokers are bonded and sometimes manage a real estate office. Either a licensed real estate sales representative or broker can assist you with purchasing and selling real estate.

2.1 Buyer representation

Buyers have a choice as to whether or not they wish to be represented by a real estate brokerage when they purchase property. A real estate brokerage or agent that represents a buyer must do what is best for the buyer. If a representation relationship is desired by the buyer, this is followed by the signing of a written buyer representation agreement which outlines and explains the services the brokerage will provide, outlines the buyer's obligations, geographical area(s), perhaps the type of property you are looking for, and establishes the fee arrangements and amount for the real estate professional's services. This is normally an exclusive relationship between the buyer and real estate brokerage for a defined period of time. The interests of the buyer client must be put ahead of the real estate professional's interests. The real estate professional (i.e., buyer's agent) is required to follow your instructions as long as they are legal and reasonable. Anything the buyer tells the agent is to be kept confidential. Information such as how much you are willing to pay for a home, your motivation, your financial information, and the like must be held in confidence. Terms and conditions and processes may vary depending on the province. Ensure you understand the agreement. Seek legal advice where appropriate.

A buyer's agent will provide information and facts that may affect your decision about a property (e.g., pricing sales and trends). Often a buyer's agent will recommend that you obtain a home inspection of the property by a third-party professional inspector who will conduct a lengthy inspection of the property and prepare a written report on the state of the property for your review. A broker (i.e., buyer's agent) is not licensed or educated to provide legal, accounting, or engineering advice. You will need to contact the appropriate professionals for these services.

2.2 Seller representation

A seller agency is a single-agency relationship whereby the seller is being represented by a real estate brokerage and the real estate brokerage must do what is best for the seller. The seller signs a listing agreement which creates the agency relationship. The seller's agent owes the seller a duty to keep information that the seller shares confidential from prospective buyers and others. In this relationship the seller's agent is still able to show a buyer the home and must be fair and honest; however, he or she does not provide any representation, only customer service to the buyer.

2.3 Multiple representation

Multiple representation (sometimes referred to as dual agency) occurs when the same brokerage is on both sides of the transaction — it represents the buyer and the seller. In this situation, the brokerage must do what is best for both the buyer and the seller. Multiple representation can exist whether one or two real estate professionals are involved in the transaction. In Ontario, it can only be practiced with the informed and written consent of both the buyers and sellers.

It is important that this relationship be properly documented as the brokerage's loyalty is divided between the buyer and the seller, who have conflicting interests. The representation agreements describe the duties and rights, as well as the limitations to those rights and duties of everyone involved.

Provincial laws and practices may vary; some have designated agency or limited dual agency. Find out laws related to the specific province and the scope of the duties and responsibilities of all parties in advance.

2.4 Customer service

A real estate brokerage can provide services to buyers and sellers without representing them; this is known as customer service. A customer service agreement explains the services which must be provided in a fair and honest manner. There is no duty of confidentiality.

If you visit a public open house without a buyer's agent, be careful not to inadvertently disclose information to the listing agent. Unless you have a buyer representation agreement with that brokerage, the salesperson may have a duty to tell the seller everything you say.

3. Individual Identification Record

In 2008, it became a national law under the Financial Transactions and Reports Analysis Centre of Canada (FINTRAC) that all buyers' and sellers' identification be requested and recorded by the real estate broker for everyone who provides funds for the purchase of real estate.

Buyers will be asked to provide their full legal name, address, date of birth, and occupation; and to provide a birth certificate, driver's licence, or passport to confirm they are who they claim to be. This information is collected and stored with the individual's real estate brokerage's office. For more information visit www.fintrac.gc.ca.

7

The Search for Your New Home

Y our next step is to complete a home buyer profile, which will help you define your must-haves or needs, your wants, and your bonus items. At this point, you should be thinking about what type of home you want to buy.

1. Make a List of What You Want and Don't Want

You probably have a general idea of whether you prefer new construction or a resale home. Begin by jotting down all the features of a home that you "must have." For example, some things you should consider include the number of bedrooms, number of bathrooms, and location (e.g., close to public or private transportation, daycare, or health care). Be specific about what you want.

It is helpful to determine a few locations such as certain cities, or even more narrowly defined as certain neighbourhoods. Considerations for a particular style, exterior finishes, or proximity to schools, highways, and trains are also important.

Next, jot down items that you would like to have, meaning they are strong preferences but not "must haves." For instance, you may want a finished basement, en suite bath, or central air. This list is usually the longest list for buyers.

Last, jot down items that you would consider a "bonus" such as appliances, in-ground pool, or acreage.

If there are any items that you absolutely do not want to have, you should list these as well (e.g., swimming pool).

2. The Different Types of Homes

There are different types of homes available, depending on your budget and preferences. Let's review the different types and styles of homes:

- **Detached house:** Is not attached to another home. It is free-standing on a lot.

- **Semidetached or link:** Two houses attached by a common wall. The common wall may be a garage, or below-ground basements, or above-ground mutual wall. Some link homes can appear detached from street level; however, they are attached by a common wall or some other form or structure below ground.

- **Townhouse:** Also referred to as an attached home or row house — these are several homes joined together.

- **Apartment:** This is a structure with a number of individual units that are attached by a common wall or walls and are also stacked on top of one another. The building can be several storeys tall.

- **Duplex:** This is a two-family dwelling or house.

Detached, semidetached, linked, and townhomes can feature either freehold or condominium ownership. Refer to Chapter 5, section **3.**, for explanation of ownership types.

It is also helpful to understand the different style concepts of the various building structures:

- **Two- or three-storey house:** As the name states, there are two or three storeys that make up the style of the house.

- **Bungalow:** This is a one-storey home. Depending on the grading of the land, occasionally this style can have an elevated or raised basement.

- **Split level:** This is a style that has several levels (i.e., three, four, or five levels). The construction of the home can be set up as a side-split, back-split, or even a front-split.

Depending on your wants, needs, budget, and geographic preference, it is ideal to view the various structures and styles as each is unique and offers different layouts and possibilities.

In some locations, your budget may, by default, dictate your options. Remember to be realistic. A good starting point to get a general idea of what you can purchase with your budget is to refer to a local newspaper which features a real estate section. Many cities and towns have real estate booklets that are published weekly and showcase a variety of properties. Leafing through these publications will give you insight into what types of properties are being offered, and at what price. You may also wish to investigate public websites that advertise properties for sale.

At this time you are ready to put your home-buying plan into action. Your home-buyer profile, combined with your pre-approved mortgage, defined budget, and geographical preferences will form the basis of your search criteria. See Worksheet 2 for an example of a home-buyer profile which you can work through (also available on the CD).

3. The Search Is On!

Now that you have contemplated your home needs and wants, and you have completed a home-buyer profile, you are ready to evaluate your home options. The following is an outline of some of the services a buyer's agent may do. Services may vary.

3.1 Do a search

A great way to get an overview of the marketplace, especially if you are considering a number of neighbourhoods, is to do a search of the available property or on a public site such as www.realtor.ca. Your broker will also execute a search of the actively listed properties using the information from your home-buyer profile on the real estate board's proprietary Multiple Listing Service® System of which they are a member.

The search results will give you the opportunity to review each of the individual properties that meet your needs, budget, and neighbourhood preferences. You will be able to see firsthand the number of homes available that meet your specific needs, wants, and budget.

Worksheet 2
Home-Buyer Profile

Name(s): _____

Address: _____ City: _____

Home #: _____ Cell #: _____ Business #: _____ Email: _____

Are you renting? When does the lease expire?
_____

Why are you considering a move?
_____

When would you like to move?
_____

How long have you been looking for a home?
_____

What neighbourhoods do you prefer?
_____

What price range?
_____

Have you been pre-approved for a mortgage?
_____

List features/options that appeal to you *(please check)*:

____ fireplace
____ pool
____ central vacuum
____ garden
____ separate workshop
____ appliances
____ lot direction
____ facilities and amenities

____ central air conditioning
____ garage
____ finished basement
____ acreage
____ hardwood floors
____ heating type

Specify any additional options:
_____
_____

Which neighbourhoods do you like? Specify geographic boundaries: _____
_____

Will you do renovations to the home? _____
How extensive? _____
_____
_____

Do any family members have special interests or requests that would be an important factor?
_____
_____
_____
_____

What accommodation type is preferred in your home?
_____

Number of bedrooms: _____
Number of bathrooms: _____
Full: _____ Partial: _____
Family room/rec room: _____

Kitchen type:
____ eat-in ____ modern ____ country

Living room: _____
_____

Dining room: _____
_____

Laundry room and location: _____
Garage and parking: _____

What type and style are preferred?

____ detached
____ link
____ freehold townhouse
____ two-storey
____ split level
____ multi level
____ Victorian
____ heritage

____ semidetached
____ townhouse
____ apartment
____ bungalow
____ ranch
____ modern
____ country

Additional comments:
_____
_____

Number of occupants to live in the home:
Adults: _____ Children: _____

Importance of proximity to public transportation highways, schools, daycare, churches, shopping:
_____
_____

When are you available to inspect homes?
_____
_____
_____

The homes will have different floor plans, features, and be in different neighbourhoods; however, all should meet your basic requirements.

Your buyer's agent will be able to educate you about neighbourhoods, amenities, home styles, time on the market, and other interesting facts. If you are looking for a home with an accessory apartment or basement suite, find out about the laws and regulations; some cities and municipalities do not allow this, but others do. Laws vary depending on the province, city, and municipality. Determine compliance requirements in advance.

Note: Sometimes buyers decide not to work with a broker, and prefer to search for a home by themselves. Often the buyers research and locate property on the Internet, visit open houses, and read the newspaper. As detailed in Chapter 6, there are different agent relationships. For example, in Ontario a listing brokerage can represent the seller and provide "customer service" to the buyer. Under this arrangement the broker must be fair and honest with the buyer; however, the buyer needs to understand that the broker is not representing him or her and may ask the buyer to sign a form confirming that he or she understands and agrees to the relationship. The brokerage discloses the relationship to the buyer and seller in writing prior to presenting an offer in Ontario. Check the rules and processes in the province in which you are buying property.

3.2 Viewing properties

The next step is for the broker to book appointments for you to view properties. As properties come on the market, your broker will notify you and set up appointments for you to view them. Timing can be important because nice homes in good areas, especially if they are well priced, sell quickly. Selecting five to seven properties that best reflect your needs, wants, budget, and geographic preferences gives you the opportunity to get a feel for layout, room sizes, features, and location.

It is important that you give the broker feedback on what you like and don't like while viewing the properties. Your broker will refine the search process based on your feedback. Having completed a home-buyer profile prior to selecting the properties to view, you have a reference point to ensure that you are looking at the properties objectively. It is very easy to like the decorating and upgrades in a property (which is also important) and to overlook some of your basic needs (e.g., number of bedrooms and closets).

Ideally you want the home search, viewing, and feedback to be completed in an objective and systematic way. It is fine to emotionally enjoy a property as long as your basic needs and goals are met. You may be surprised at what you are able to buy (both positively and negatively), which may require modifying your needs and wants, or possibly location. Once you have been in the marketplace a few times you will begin to get a good sense of the types of homes that are available in your price range and geographic areas.

Consider commenting on features and items that you like about the homes and rank these features in order of their importance. Ask yourself why you like or dislike features; this helps you to focus on what is important. The broker should be knowledgeable about the inventory on the market and he or she can make suggestions. Sometimes the broker may offer alternatives that you had not considered.

Try to visualize yourself living in the property. Walk around the back of the yard or stand on the balcony (if applicable). What do you see and how do you feel?

Print a few copies of Worksheet 3 from the CD so that you can use it to make comments about each home you visit.

3.3 How long will it take to find a home?

The time it takes to find a home will vary for each person. It depends on market conditions, the number of properties that are on the market, and the availability of the type of property the buyer is seeking. The broker will be able to educate you on these details. Additionally your broker will review how long properties, in general, remain on the market. Sometimes it can be for a short time (e.g., one to two days), or it can be longer (e.g., weeks or months).

Sometimes a home that is overpriced relative to similar homes will remain on the market for weeks or even months. Homes that may have undesirable features such as poor location, poor view, bad condition, obsolete design, or some other negative feature may take some time to sell as well. Over time these properties may be reduced in price to attract attention.

You will want to know what the average time is for a home to sell in your choice neighbourhood because this will help you determine your offer strategy with respect to price and other terms.

Worksheet 3
Home-Buyer Checklist

Address: _____ Price: _____

Overall impression: Excellent _____ Good _____ Satisfactory _____ Poor _____

Age of home: _____ Is the home: New construction: _____ Resale: _____

Type of home: Detached _____ Semidetached _____ Townhome _____ Link _____
Duplex _____ Condominium _____ Freehold _____ Condo ____

Expenses: Taxes _____ Condo fees _____ Includes _____

Size of lot: Excellent _____ Good _____ Satisfactory _____ Poor _____
Fenced yard: Yes _____ No _____
Deck: Yes _____ No _____
Patio: Yes _____ No _____

View (condo): Excellent _____ Good _____ Satisfactory _____ Poor _____

Number of bedrooms: 1 ____ 2 _____ 3 _____ 4 _____ 5 _____ 6 _____
Number of closets: 1 ____ 2 _____ 3 _____ 4 _____ 5 _____ 6 _____
Number of bathrooms: 1 ____ 2 _____ 3 _____ 4 _____ 5 _____ 6 _____
En suite bathroom: Yes _____ No _____ Separate shower _____ Separate tub _____
Two-piece bath _____ Main level _____ Basement _____
Other _____
Number of showers: 1 ____ 2 _____ 3 ____

Basement: Finished _____ Partially finished _____ Unfinished _____ N/A ____
Walkout _____ Raised _____ High ceilings _____
Storage _____ Workshop _____

Accessory suite: Rented Y _____ N _____ Size _____ Number of bedrooms ____
Is it legal? _____

Exterior of home: Brick _____ Concrete _____ Aluminum siding _____ Wood _____
Vinyl siding _____ Stone _____ Combination _____
Roof: Shingles _____ Tile _____ Steel _____ Shaker _____ Age ____

Foundation: Concrete _____ Block _____ Wood _____

Heating: Gas _____ Electric _____ Oil _____ Wood _____ Age _____
Air conditioning: Central _____ Window _____

Garage: Single _____ Two-car _____ Three-car _____ Four-car_____
Carport _____ No garage ____
Private driveway: Yes _____ Shared _____ Laneway _____ None _____

Parking (condo): One parking space _____ Two parking spaces _____
Three parking spaces ____

Worksheet 3 — Continued

Locker (condo): Separate locker _____ In unit _____

Kitchen: Eat-in _____ Pantry _____ Countertop type _____ Cupboards _____
Appliances: Fridge _____ Stove _____ Dishwasher _____ Microwave _____
            Other _____

Separate dining room: Yes _____ No _____
Family room: Yes _____ No _____

Laundry room: Main level _____ Basement _____ Second floor _____
              Washer _____ Dryer _____

Office/Den: Yes _____ No _____ Location _____

Type of flooring: Hardwood _____ Parquet _____ Carpet _____ Other _____

Kitchen and bathroom flooring: Ceramic tile _____ Porcelain _____ Travertine _____
                         Vinyl _____ Other_____

Security system: Yes _____ No _____ Monitored _____ Leased _____

Hot water tank: Owned _____ Leased _____ Tankless _____

Swimming pool: Yes _____ No _____ Heated _____ Above ground _____
              In-ground _____ Vinyl _____ Concrete _____
Hot tub: Yes _____ No _____

Location — number of kilometres to the following:
    Work _____ Bus _____ Train _____
    School _____ Shopping _____ Recreation _____
    Babysitter _____ Hospital _____ Doctor _____
    Dentist _____ Park _____ Church _____
    Police _____ Fire _____ Vet _____
    Other _____

Generally speaking, you should be able to locate a suitable property in a few weeks to couple of months. Your broker will have a system with which to notify you each time an appropriate home becomes available, and set up an appointment for you to view it.

3.4 Market data

During the course of the search and viewing process, your broker can provide you with valuable information such as sales stats, sales trends, listing-to-sales ratios, and time on the market for the properties you consider. Be mindful of area- and product-specific data because this can vary relative to the overall marketplace. For example, the overall market data in a province or a city may reflect a balanced marketplace; however, neighbourhood- or product-specific data may indicate a shortage of inventory.

The neighbourhood-specific data can be as narrow as a few streets that are perhaps close to a high-demand school. Another example may be certain floor plans and a shortage of specific high-demand models; high-demand homes can be greeted with multiple offers shortly after a property is listed for sale. Buyers' agents can access the sales statistics as well as other important data.

4. What Type of Economic Market Cycle Is the Real Estate Market Experiencing?

It is important to understand the different types of real estate markets; that is, buyer's market, seller's market, and balanced market. Knowing the type of cycle the real estate market is experiencing is important because it will play a role in how you locate and negotiate your home purchase.

The overall state of the economy affects the real estate market. A healthy economy creates an optimistic mood in which consumers feel good and tend to purchase big-ticket items such as homes, vehicles, and furniture. Conversely, if the economy is unhealthy or challenged, consumers shy away from spending, and as such demand for homes and other big-ticket items is low. This can affect pricing and inventory levels for homes.

Once you locate the home you want, how you negotiate your offer to purchase, which clauses and conditions, and the strategies you use will depend on the real estate market at the time. The following sections take a closer look at market conditions and cycles.

4.1 Seller's market

The seller's market is a marketplace that has more buyers than homes available to buy. As price is influenced by supply and demand, increased demand normally correlates with an increase in prices. Often in this type of marketplace you will be competing with other buyers for the same home.

Buyers may need to make quick decisions in a seller's market and, in many cases, there are multiple offers from more than one buyer at the same time. Usually buyers like to start an offer with a lower offer than the list price and even include conditions such as home inspection and financing in their initial offer, and prefer to negotiate with the seller. In a seller's market, this can be difficult, if not impossible, because the seller may have more than one buyer making an offer. Naturally the seller will review all offers and accept or work with the best one. This can be a difficult market for first-time buyers to work in; however, in high-demand areas and hot markets, this can be the reality.

4.2 Buyer's market

A buyer's market is the opposite of a seller's market whereby there is a greater number or supply of homes available than there are buyers. This is a favourable market for buyers because they can take their time. Also, their negotiating power is higher than in a seller's market. A buyer can present a lower offer, possibly even have conditions such as home inspection, financing, status certificate review and approval, and other conditions relevant to the property or area.

In prolonged buyer's markets, prices tend to fall as motivated sellers reduce their prices from their listed competition in an attempt to motivate buyers to consider their property over the competition. Of course, the downfall in this type of market is that buyers worry whether prices will continue to decline and where the bottom may be. There is no crystal ball. Look at purchasing a home as a long-term investment and consider the benefits that are derived from home ownership.

4.3 Balanced market

A balanced market is an ideal marketplace; the supply of homes on the market is in balance with the number of buyers seeking homes. Prices are stable and there aren't the hot and cold emotions as in the other two markets. Motivation of the seller and buyer is more likely to dictate the end result of negotiations, rather than the marketplace.

4.4 What type of marketplace are you currently experiencing?

The marketplace you are in will eventually become obvious given the sales and inventory. It is wise to ask your broker for market and sales advice and statistics. Occasionally, situations occur whereby the market is in balance or even somewhat slower in a given city; however, an isolated neighbourhood (which could be a four- to five-block radius) can be very hot or very cold compared to the overall marketplace.

4.5 Seasonal cycles

Traditionally you will find that spring and fall have the most amount of inventory on the market to view. December and January usually have the least inventory. This happens to coincide with winter, Christmas holidays, and the school year.

Most resale home sales have a 60-day closing, which means if you purchased a home in February or March, the closing or completion would be in April, May, or even June. Although closing dates are negotiable, the average is 60 days.

Given that the school year ends in June, most families like to move in June or July — after the school year has finished and prior to the start of the new school year in September. Normally sellers put their homes on the market at the end of February through to March, April, and May anticipating a June, July, or even August closing date. From a buyer's perspective, you will have more homes to choose from in this time period; however, you may also have more buyers to compete with depending on the type of marketplace you are experiencing.

The second most popular time for sellers to list their homes for sale is in the fall (i.e., September, October, November). Sellers and buyers with children like to time their move with the Christmas holidays. Again a buyer will have more inventory to choose from, but may also have more buyers to compete with for the same home.

From a buyer's point of view, purchasing a home in December or January will give the buyer more leverage as the marketplace tends to be slower at this time (there are fewer homes available for sale to choose from, but there are also fewer buyers). Understand that most December and January purchases will have a February or March closing date, when it can be cold or snowy. The benefit is that often you will have more leverage as a buyer.

In Québec, July 1 is known as "moving day"; it is tradition, but not law for leases to start and end on this day. As a result it is difficult to book a moving vehicle or moving company, and rates are significantly higher due to demand. As a buyer you are not required to close your purchase on July 1; it is important, however, to check with a broker, lawyer, or notary regarding closing dates and registration requirements as laws and practices in Québec may be different.

It is time well spent to investigate the type of marketplace you are buying in as well as to understand the seasonality of sales in your chosen area. Understanding this will help you decide on your negotiating strategy. For example, if there are more homes than average available, and fewer buyers, your offer can likely begin with a lower price and different terms and conditions than in a reverse marketplace.

Sometimes there are exceptions; for instance, there have been balanced markets overall in a given city, while at the same time there may be a very high demand for detached bungalows and few available. In this case, despite the balanced marketplace overall, the detached bungalows may experience the equivalent of a seller's market for that specific product type. Another example is the overall market may be a seller's market in general; however, due to several new condominium buildings under construction, this product type may have an abundance of inventory enabling a buyer to experience the equivalent of a buyer's market with this product type.

An experienced broker will be able to educate and assist you with understanding the market, product trends, and inventory available.

8

The Agreement of Purchase and Sale

Congratulations! You have found the perfect home! Now the time has come to make an offer to purchase it. The offer, which is also known as the agreement of purchase and sale, is a written agreement that spells out the details (i.e., the terms and conditions that are agreed upon between the buyers and sellers). If the agreement is accepted and signed by all parties to the transaction (and the conditions are met and satisfied), it is a firm and legally binding contract.

If you decide to purchase a new home from a builder, you will most likely be required to sign a builder's agreement of purchase and sale. The builder's agreement is often several pages in length and is drafted by the builder's lawyer. It is important to have your lawyer review the agreement, ideally prior to signing. Remember, having a lawyer review the agreement is for your protection. If this is not possible (perhaps you locate and want to purchase a property on a Friday evening or weekend and the lawyer is not available to review the offer), consider including a condition in your agreement stating that the sale is conditional on your lawyer's review and approval, which provides you with the ability to void the agreement and have any deposit funds returned in full, should your lawyer advise you of terms and conditions that are unacceptable to you that the seller is unwilling to remove or modify. This way you can still negotiate the offer and then have your lawyer review the agreement on Monday. Have your lawyer provide the proper wording for the "condition on lawyer approval" clause, in advance, in anticipation that you may need to use it in an offer should you be in this situation.

Understand that an agreement of purchase and sale is an important contract which contains numerous terms, conditions, and clauses. Once signed by the buyer and seller (assuming all conditions are fulfilled) it becomes a binding, legal agreement.

This chapter will illustrate the process of completing and presenting an offer. It reviews common items and clauses included in many agreements. It is not meant to be an extensive discussion of every term, condition, or clause that is or can be in an agreement. Each individual purchase is different and requires different terms and clauses. Additionally, provinces have different laws which may require different processes, terms, conditions, and clauses. The purpose of this chapter is to give you an overview of some of the things that you may want to consider. An experienced real estate professional is knowledgeable about the contents of the agreement of purchase and sale that is available from his or her office or local real estate board. However, remember your real estate professional cannot give you legal advice; that is the job of your lawyer. It is important to seek appropriate legal assistance and advice in the province in which you are planning to purchase a home.

With respect to a resale agreement of purchase and sale, your real estate professional (i.e., buyer's agent) will complete the agreement for you to review. Using a pre-printed resale agreement of purchase and sale form, your real estate professional will fill in the blanks where appropriate. These pre-printed agreements contain terms and clauses that are common in your province, which means they have likely been reviewed by your local or provincial real estate board or association. Note that laws and processes vary depending on the province. Despite the fact the pre-printed terms and clauses may be common in your province, this doesn't necessarily mean they are all appropriate for you. Make sure you understand and are in agreement with what you are signing; ideally have your lawyer read the agreement prior to signing it.

1. What Is Included in an Agreement of Purchase and Sale

The following information is usually included in an agreement of purchase and sale:

- Seller's and buyer's legal names.

- Legal municipal address and lot size (where appropriate). This is the legal description, including lot and plan number, which is specific to the property.

- Price you are offering.

- Amount of deposit, which is not the same as a down payment, although it forms part of your down payment. This is a *good faith* deposit to show you are serious about the purchase. Often the deposit is held in trust by the listing broker or a lawyer (depending on the province and individual situation) and is credited towards the purchase price on closing. The amount of the deposit varies. The amount is agreed upon between the buyer and seller. There is no set amount, but there may be geographic norms. Often, it is in the 5 percent of purchase range. In some cases (if funds are locked into investments) the buyer may pay the deposit in installments over time or upon waiving certain conditions. Discuss the amount with your broker. Be specific about when it is due (i.e., upon acceptance of offer, or within 24 hours of acceptance).

- Closing date, which is the day when you complete the transaction, exchange funds, pay closing-related expenses, register documents (e.g., transfer title), and get the keys to your home. This date is negotiated and agreed upon by the buyer and seller. Sometimes the closing date is also the possession date; sometimes this is not the case.

- Included and excluded items such as appliances, window coverings, and electric light fixtures. You will need to understand the difference between what is considered a *fixture* and a *chattel*. Fixtures are permanent items that stay with the property. Occasionally, certain fixtures are excluded or are unclear as to whether they stay such as a dining room chandelier, attached shelving, or window blinds. Chattels are movable items or personal property such as a microwave, washer, dryer, and window coverings. Some items (chattels or fixtures) may be leased such as a hot water tank, a furnace, or an alarm system. Be specific and list everything that you wish to be included and excluded and whether it is owned or you are assuming a lease and at what cost. It is wise to specify the make, model, and serial number of appliances, which helps prevent any unnecessary surprises.

- Irrevocable date, or date and time the offer is open for review and consideration by the seller to decide to either accept, reject, or send the offer back with a counteroffer. If the offer is signed by the buyer under seal this means the buyer cannot change his or her mind about it until the irrevocable date and time expire. Ensure you understand the meaning of this clause.

- Title search (requisition date) to examine the title. In Ontario the requisition date (also known as the search title date) is the date that your lawyer has to do a variety of searches. Usually the lawyer requests certain documents and examines title by this date and if the lawyer finds any issues, he or she needs to notify the seller's lawyer by the requisition date and the seller must attempt to correct the problems before closing. If problems cannot be corrected speak with your lawyer (refer to Chapter 10). You will want to make sure your lawyer has ample time to do the appropriate searches and requisitions.

- Condominium agreements include other items such as the amount of the monthly condominium/strata/maintenance fee and what is included with it (e.g., electricity, water, common elements, building insurance) as well as other condominium-related items such as parking, storage locker, and clauses regarding the condominium corporation. Resale condominium agreements of purchase and sale are different than freehold agreements.

The buyer's agent may add additional clauses and conditions on a separate schedule that are important and relevant to you and your transaction. Every real estate transaction is different. The agreement of purchase and sale should include clauses to protect your interests.

You may include conditions regarding obtaining financing; home inspection; status or estoppel certificate for condominium properties; lawyer review and approval; insurance confirmation; review and approval of a plan of survey; and septic, well, and water tests. The relevant conditions will depend on the province; location of the property (i.e., urban, rural, country); type of property; age of property; and other customs, processes, laws, and issues that are important to you and your specific purchase. It is important to discuss these with your real estate professional and lawyer. If the included conditions are not met or satisfied within the specified time, your offer becomes null and void and you usually have the right to get your deposit returned (make sure this is noted in your conditions — proper wording is important to ensure a clean break from the agreement).

Normally, a buyer's agent will review and present data on properties in the same area as the subject property that are similar in size, features, lot size, condition, and age that are currently available for sale (you may have viewed some of these comparable homes), as well as similar or comparable homes that have sold within the last six months. The buyer agent will make pricing adjustments for features and upgrades that may differ from the subject property (e.g., finished basement, new kitchen or bathroom, larger lot). Given the condition of the home, other inventory in the area, market conditions, and other possible variables, the buyer's agent will review and discuss this data with you and be able to determine a reasonable range of value for the subject property. This is known as a Comparative Market Analysis (CMA). After reviewing the data, you will be able to determine whether the seller's listing price is fair, overpriced or underpriced, and you will be able to decide on a price you wish to offer.

Of course, there is often *subjective* value attached to real estate. This is a personal value you may attach to the home and it may be different for each buyer. It is difficult to attach value to subjective emotion or desire.

The agreement of purchase and sale should contain everything that is important about the home and the transaction including specifying items that will come with the home. The agreement of purchase and sale should be clear and concise so as to avoid misunderstandings or problems in the future. Keep in mind it is a legal agreement and it is very important that you understand what you are agreeing to. Always seek legal advice.

Assuming the seller accepts and any and all conditions are met and removed within the specified time frame, it is at that time that your offer becomes a firm deal and the home is considered sold. The wording of conditions is technical and particular to the province, property, and transaction involved; it deserves a discussion and review with your lawyer and real estate professional.

The process of completing an agreement of purchase and sale, reviewing statistical sales data, determining a price, negotiating the offer, and other factors will vary depending on the type of agency relationship that you have with a real estate professional as well as the laws of the province in which you are purchasing your home. Be sure that you understand whether the real estate professional is acting as a buyer's agent and is representing you, or whether you have another type of relationship with limited duties. (See Chapter 6 for agency relationship definitions.) If you are not working with a real estate professional, the process will be different.

Do not sign anything that you don't understand and always ask for clarity. Remember, it is a legal document you are signing. It is important that you understand and are satisfied with the terms, conditions, and contents of the agreement because it is binding once it is signed.

2. Negotiating the Offer

Once you have signed the agreement of purchase and sale, the next step is for your real estate professional to present the offer to the seller or seller's agent. During the irrevocable time frame, the seller has three choices: he or she can accept the offer, reject it, or make a counteroffer.

Sometimes the seller makes a counteroffer to you — perhaps changing the price or closing date, removing chattels, or adding different terms. A counteroffer by the seller indicates the seller has an interest in your offer but is not happy with some items in your offer. If you are not satisfied with the seller's counteroffer, you can re-submit another counteroffer for the seller to consider. This process is known as *negotiation* and continues until both parties come to an agreement, or until one party ends the negotiation.

Occasionally, your initial offer may be rejected with no counter-offer from the seller. If this is the case, try to find out why this occurred. You can always submit another offer.

In a hot real estate market, especially if there are limited homes available for sale, a buyer may find himself or herself having to compete with other buyers for the same home. This is known as multiple offers; this may be an ideal situation for the seller, however, the buyer needs to proceed prudently and take precautions. In this situation it is usually difficult for a negotiation process to occur as the seller normally reviews all offers and may accept or work with the best one or may decide not to accept any.

In hot markets, in a multiple-offer situation, often buyers come in with their best offer, not only in terms of price, but other terms and conditions as well. Normally, offers are presented to the seller in a closed bid process, meaning the buyers are not aware of what other buyers are offering. It is not normally done in an auction process. Sellers can ask that all offers be faxed or delivered to the seller's agent. Buyers sometimes tighten or remove conditions in an attempt to make an offer more appealing to the seller. Proceed with caution. If you remove or exclude conditions such as a home inspection, financing, legal approval, and status certificate review (for condominiums) and offer a firm (no conditions) agreement which is accepted by the sellers, you now have a firm and binding contract. Make sure you are comfortable as this can be a risky thing to do.

On occasion, buyers are able to arrange a home inspection, prior to the seller reviewing the multiple offers, so at least the buyer will have an understanding of the condition of the home. Otherwise, you may want to consider including a home inspection condition for one or two days. If you are pre-approved for a mortgage, depending on the strength of financing amongst other factors, your mortgage professional may confirm and advise you that it is fine to proceed without a finance condition. Ideally, get this in writing. Make sure there are no limitations or exceptions. Remember the lender will probably complete an appraisal of the property and may only be willing to lend up to a certain percentage of the value. Often the status certificate (for condominiums) is available and you have the opportunity to review the documents, the financials, bylaws, and rules and regulations in advance of the multiple offer presentation. Having your ducks in a row and being prepared for this type of situation is helpful. Once the seller has reviewed the offers he or she will usually choose one to work with or accept.

Sometimes the home sells for more than it was listed. Occasionally, there are situations when multiple offers are similar, or are not acceptable; in this case the seller's agent may ask all buyers to submit new offers and allow the buyers the opportunity to modify their offers and resubmit.

Assuming real estate professionals are involved in the transaction (i.e., it is not a private sale), in Ontario there are rules regarding how multiple offers must be handled especially if multiple representation is involved. Check with your real estate professional and lawyer about the laws pertinent to your province. Try not to get too emotional or to overextend yourself. You don't want to get caught up in the heat of the multiple-offer situation and regret it afterwards.

If the negotiation process is successful, and your offer is accepted, you may have an obligation to complete certain conditions (e.g., home inspection, financing, or review of offer by lawyer) within a specified time frame.

Usually, upon seller acceptance of the offer, the buyer will be required to submit a deposit as agreed to in the offer. The amount of the deposit varies depending on what is agreed to. Depending on the situation, the deposit is normally held in trust by the listing broker, the selling broker, a lawyer, or the builder. Who holds the deposit is also specified in the agreement. The deposit shows good faith, is held in trust, and credited towards the purchase price on closing. In the event that conditions are not satisfied and the agreement is determined to be voided, appropriate wording needs to have been included in the agreement so that the buyer's deposit will be returned to the buyer, without deduction and within a reasonable time. Check with your agent or lawyer for the proper wording to protect your interests.

Occasionally, the deposit is provided in graduated payments over time with a certain amount provided upon acceptance of an offer, and a further deposit provided at some point in the future. This is often the case with new homes. This needs to be spelled out specifically in the agreement including the amounts due and when.

If you are purchasing a home where there are no real estate professionals involved (i.e., private sale), you are urged to seek legal advice. Completing an agreement of purchase and sale, presenting and negotiating the offer with the seller directly, determining price, closing, and many other important items need to be properly spelled out and agreed upon. You will also need to determine who will hold the deposit and how to deal with conditions.

Sometimes buyers want to obtain a better price when dealing directly with the seller because they know the seller is not paying real estate fees. This can be a hurdle to overcome. Additionally, it may be an emotional process for the buyer and seller to negotiate with one another as both want to get the best deal and there is no third party (e.g., lawyer or real estate professional) to handle the negotiations.

Proceed with caution in that kind of case. These comments are not made in order to persuade you to work with a real estate professional; they are to give you an understanding of what you may encounter. It is recommended that you always understand the terms of any agreement and seek legal advice before signing any contract.

9

The Home Inspection

It is common practice for real estate professionals to recommend that a potential buyer have a home inspected by a home inspector prior to finalizing the deal. The home may look great visually; however, do you know what is behind the walls, under the foundation, in the roof, and below the ground? Most buyers are not trained to find major operating and structural problems, which could become unexpected, expensive, and unwanted issues in the future.

A common condition or contingency in an agreement of purchase and sale is that of having a home inspection by a qualified or registered home inspector. Sometimes, in a hot market, where there are multiple offers on a given property, to make the offer more appealing to the seller, the buyer decides not to include a home inspection condition. Think twice about this; although costly and time consuming, especially when faced with the pressure of a multiple offer situation, it is prudent to complete a home inspection prior to offer presentation time.

Occasionally, a seller will have a pre-home inspection completed by a home inspector when the home is put on the market. Although a pre-inspection report may contain valuable information, keep in mind that it was prepared for the seller. Ask if the seller has completed a property disclosure statement and request a copy. Ultimately, you need to feel comfortable and be knowledgeable about the home and the buying process. Different homes and types of markets present different issues and options. Discuss this with your real estate professional and lawyer.

Having a home inspected by a qualified or registered home inspector gives you the knowledge and comfort of knowing what to expect. You can make prudent and informed decisions about the cost of anticipated immediate and future repairs or updates. Remember, this is likely your single largest investment and you will want to minimize surprises.

1. What Is Covered in a Home Inspection?

A home inspection is like performing a "physical" on a property; you will find out what condition the home is in. There is no such thing as a perfect home — and the home inspection doesn't give it a pass or fail grade. The home inspection is not an appraisal of the market value of the home. A home inspection provides you with a detailed report describing the condition of the home, and information on maintaining the home. If it turns out that the home is in worse condition than you thought, or if you discover any defects, assuming the home inspection condition is worded in such a way, the buyer will be able to cancel the deal and have your deposit returned or, alternatively, you may decide to renegotiate the deal.

Proper legal wording is imperative to assure a clean break from the transaction and your deposit returned in full. Consult with your lawyer regarding the appropriate legal clause to ensure this protection.

The wording of the home inspection condition clause is important. The home inspection condition should clearly state what the condition is for, who pays for the inspection (normally the buyer), and for what length of time it is conditional (e.g., three business days). The condition should also indicate how the condition is fulfilled and relied upon; for example, if the inspection reveals deficiencies, how do you rely on the condition to cancel the deal?

Many sellers, especially those with well-cared-for homes, think there is nothing wrong with their home and a home inspection that reveals deficiencies can be a shock to them. If your home inspection reveals deficiencies that need addressing, it does not mean you have to cancel your deal; rather you may decide to obtain pricing estimates on the cost to repair the deficiencies, present this information to the seller's agent, and attempt to renegotiate your deal (prior to removing the condition on home inspection). Sometimes the seller will agree to a price reduction so that you can complete the necessary repairs. Alternatively, the seller may agree to have the work completed at his or her expense prior to closing. If the seller is willing to complete the repairs at his or her expense, you will want to insert a clause ensuring that the work is done in a professional manner (ideally by a professional), and that you have the ability to inspect the repairs prior to closing.

An experienced buyer's agent or lawyer will be able to provide the appropriate legal clauses and renegotiate the deal where appropriate. Remember, any renegotiations or agreements of work to be completed or re-inspected should be specific and in writing.

In a hot seller's market, the above strategy may not work; the seller may simply move on to the next prospective buyer. Ultimately, it will be your decision (as a buyer) how to proceed, but at least you will be aware of the necessary work and liability you are taking on after you have completed a home inspection and obtained estimates from independent contractors and tradespeople on costs to repair or replace deficiencies.

2. What Is the Role of the Home Inspector?

Normally a home inspector visually inspects all accessible systems and components of the home, including but not limited to structure and foundation, plumbing, electrical, roofs and attics, basements, heating and air conditioning systems, water heater, ceilings, insulation, walls, windows, floors and doors, and the property. You will also find that the home inspection gives you an excellent opportunity to gain in-depth knowledge about your prospective property.

Depending on the type of home being inspected along with its individual components, sometimes separate inspections or certifications are obtained for wood burning fireplaces (WETT certificates), septic tanks and systems, well and water tests, swimming pools, wood destroying insects (WDI), and mould. As an example, what is the source of water for the property (e.g., well)? You may want or even need to obtain a certificate of potability; some lenders may require this certificate. The process used to test water involves providing a series of samples of water over a specific time frame that are analyzed by a lab to ensure it is suitable for consumption.

In the case of older homes, an inspector may suspect the presence of lead paint, urea formaldehyde, or asbestos which may require testing to verify. Termites are another problem that could be identified in homes. Depending on the location of the home, the inspector may also check for radon gas.

The Canadian Association of Home and Property Inspectors (CAHPI) as well as some provincial home inspections associations give standards as to what a home inspector should do as a minimum. According to some of the associations, the home inspector's scope of the inspection is limited to a visual inspection of *accessible* systems and components. The inspector is not expected or required to move personal property or dismantle anything to get access. The home inspector is expected to determine if any of the systems or components of the home are deficient or near the end of their life cycle and why.

According to CAHPI, the home inspection profession is unregulated except in British Columbia and Alberta. CAHPI inspectors can use the designation of Registered Home Inspector or "RHI" if they have met the requirements of the provincial and regional associations. This designation identifies the inspector as a member of the Canadian Association of Home and Property Inspectors. The provincial and regional associations are self-regulating. Many home-inspection companies are reputable and have adopted association standards; however, there are no guarantees that the inspector you hire is experienced with good credentials. You can start by asking family and friends if they have used a home inspector with which they were happy. The CAHPI website (www.cahpi.ca) offers a directory and links to home inspectors.

Contact the home inspector or firm and ask about the inspector's credentials and experience. Some home inspectors have backgrounds with education and training such as architects or engineers. Obviously, the more education, training, and experience that a home inspector has, the better.

It is also a good idea to ask the home inspector if he or she is a member of a professional association — whether it is a membership with CAHPI or a provincial association. You can contact the provincial or territorial or national association to check that the inspector is in fact registered. Being a member of an association provides no guarantees; however, most associations have a set of standards and code of conduct, which means the inspector member is supposed to abide by the association's rules and conduct guidelines. According to CAHPI, it has appointed a national steering committee and it is working on preparing applications for accreditation.

Ask the home inspector about liability with respect to the home inspection. Does he or she have errors and omissions insurance or professional liability insurance? Usually this type of insurance covers financial loss caused by an error, an omission, or a mistake. Find out if the home inspector will provide you with a written report (most do) of the home inspection and when will you get this report. Some home inspectors have fine print in their reports that limits liability, so ask about this when you hire the inspector and understand any limitations prior to the inspection. Inquire about the amount of detail that will be in the report and whether or not the report is a boilerplate document.

2.1 Insulation

Ask what type of insulation is in the home as some types of insulation in attics may contain a form of asbestos that could be carcinogenic. Asbestos can pose health risks when fibres are present in the air that we breathe; when inhaled asbestos fibres can lodge in the lungs and over time may result in lung problems. According to Health Canada, if asbestos fibres are enclosed, tightly bound, or isolated in a product there are no significant health risks.

Vermiculite is one of four types of loose-fill insulation used in homes. Vermiculite is a mica-like mineral that is fire resistant and has good insulation qualities. Recently concerns have emerged that some of the vermiculate insulation installed in homes may contain asbestos. If the insulation is sealed behind wallboards and floorboards, isolated in an attic, or otherwise kept from exposure to the interior of the home, there is currently no evidence of risk to human health. If the insulation contains asbestos, however, and it is disturbed, it could release fibres into the air. At this time vermiculite insulation is not banned and it is not considered a latent defect.

In the past, another form of insulation, called Urea Formaldehyde Foam Insulation (UFFI) was banned due to suspected health risks. There were government programs to help owners remove UFFI from their homes. Although not in effect now, CMHC previously required a disclosure from the seller as to whether the seller was aware if there ever had been UFFI in the home. No disclosure is required by CMHC regarding the presence of vermiculite insulation. Ensure that you have a discussion with your home inspector regarding insulation.

2.2 Marijuana grow operations

It is also important that the home be checked to ensure there is no evidence of a marijuana grow operation. Grow ops in homes and other dwellings can result in severe mould growth and cause structural and electrical damage. A number of grow ops have been located in basements of homes. No community or home type is immune — grow ops are operating throughout Canada. Marijuana grow ops use large amounts of electricity and water. Homes often undergo renovations such as a redirection of hydro or electrical lines and tampering with the meters that measure water and electricity consumption, so as to pass the costs on to other consumers and avoid detection. These home renovations, especially with respect to electrical wiring, can create fire hazards. Sometimes the furnace is re-vented to circulate the air for the marijuana plants; this can circulate toxic fumes from the furnace back into the home. Toxic fertilizers or chemicals are used to enhance plant growth; there can also be a build-up of poisonous gases from the chemical nutrients which could cause an explosion. Mould presents a health issue and increases the risk of upper respiratory diseases. If you are concerned that the home you are having inspected may have been a grow op, you may decide to have a separate mould inspection completed by a mould specialist.

Repairs due to grow ops can cost many thousands of dollars. The foundation of the home can be compromised, moisture accumulation may cause structural damage, uncovered outdoor electrical wires near power meters are dangerous; these illegal operations can create safety concerns for the whole neighbourhood.

Items to look for to identify a grow op include mould in corners, painted concrete floors in the basement, marks on the floor where pots may have been, stains around the soffit that continue along the siding, holes from screws in the wall, electrical meter damage, and modified wiring. While viewing a home, also check whether there is heavy condensation on the inside windows, or discolouration on the roof.

Homes that had, even for a short period of time, marijuana grow ops can create health and safety issues for a buyer. Obtaining property insurance may be difficult if not impossible. Ask the seller if he or she is aware of any defects (i.e., latent or patent — those defects that would be obvious to a layperson, and those which wouldn't be). There may be an obligation for the seller to disclose material latent defects that are known or should be known by the seller; otherwise, the seller could be liable for damages to the buyer for costs of repairs to make the property fit for habitation. Some real estate professionals also include a clause in the agreement of purchase and sale that in effect has the seller confirm or represent that the home, to the best of the seller's knowledge, has not been used for purposes of a grow op. Speak with your real estate professional and lawyer about appropriate wording. It is prudent to ensure that your home inspector look for potential signs or evidence of a marijuana grow operation.

2.3 Accessory apartments

Another area to investigate during the home inspection involves secondary suites or accessory apartments (e.g., basement apartments). Generally speaking, a secondary suite or an accessory apartment is a self-contained unit, which may or may not be rented, on a detached or semidetached home — many of which are located in the basement of a home.

Discuss with the home inspector whether these suites comply with fire and building codes, along with a host of other possible requirements. The suite may need to be retrofitted in order to comply. An inspection by the fire department may be required.

Provincial and municipal or city governments may have laws or regulations regarding secondary suites such as zoning and parking. They may even be prohibited in some cities.

Check with your insurance company about their requirements. Find out the facts in advance. There may be fines or penalties for non-compliance.

2.4 Attend the home inspection

It is advisable you attend the home inspection and literally walk around the home with the inspector during the inspection, which usually takes about three hours. Normally the home inspector will inform and educate you about the components and systems of the home, their age, and condition, as well as advise you if any are in need of repair or replacement. You will see any problems visually and become familiar with the home. Many home inspectors provide maintenance information along with other tips on how to keep your home in good operating condition.

During the inspection, it is a good time to ask questions, especially if you don't understand something the inspector is reporting. If the home you are having inspected is vacant, ask your real estate professional to ensure that the power and utilities are on during the inspection. The home inspector should not quote prices on the cost to repair or replace items or issues, but he or she should inform you of the problem and the potential severity. If repairs are recommended, consider getting a couple of quotes from a contractor or professional.

2.5 The home inspection report

At the end of the home inspection (or usually within 24 hours), the home inspector should provide you with a report that gives a summary and outline of the inspection. It should highlight deficiencies and recommendations to remedy the problems. Some reports include digital photos as well as general information on structural and operating components and maintenance suggestions.

It is sometimes difficult to know about a latent defect as it is normally not readily apparent, possibly hidden, and as such cannot be discovered by a reasonably thorough inspection of the home. Patent defects are flaws that are generally clear, obvious, detectable, and not hidden, such as broken windows, cracked tiles, and missing roof shingles. Ask the seller or seller's agent if he or she has knowledge of any latent or patent defects. Sellers are obligated to disclose material latent defects they know about or should have known about, that could make the home unsafe or unfit for human habitation.

A buyer may decide to make a claim against a seller for latent defects that are later discovered; the buyer may make an argument or presumption that the seller misrepresented. The seller would be required to prove that he or she could not have possibly known about the defect. Proving the seller was aware of the defect could be difficult; however, if it can be successfully proven that the seller misrepresented, concealed, or lied, especially if he or she was asked, the seller may be liable for damages to the buyer for the cost to remedy the property.

Generally speaking the inspection is broken down into major categories:

- Is the home dry? Are there any cracks or leaks in the basement? Is there any evidence of leakage from the roof? Did you check under the sinks in the kitchen, bathrooms, and laundry room?

- Are there safety issues such as electrical wiring and a properly working furnace (e.g., is there the potential for cracked heat exchanger or carbon monoxide poisoning)?

- Are structural and operating systems working properly and do they comply with building codes? Some home inspectors offer information about operating and maintenance efficiencies and tasks.

Occasionally, the federal and provincial governments offer grants and other incentives for homeowners to change and upgrade some components. The EnerGuide Retrofit grant to homeowners who renovate their homes to improve the energy efficiency rating of the home and the Residential Rehabilitation Assistance, a federal program provides financial assistance to renovate or repair housing that needs to be brought up to basic health and safety standards are examples. For additional information on how to qualify for these programs contact National Resources Canada at 613-995-2943 or 1-800-387-2000 for the EnerGuide Retrofit grant, and CMHC at 1-800-704-6488 for the Residential Rehabilitation Assistance program. Ask your real estate professional and home inspector if they are aware of any current programs. You can also check the CMHC and Natural Resources Canada websites. Any grant or credit will help offset your expense to upgrade or replace a component.

An inspection is not technically exhaustive and may not detect every issue or flaw. There is also generally a list of exclusions such as survey and boundaries, zoning and permit compliance, soil conditions, easements and rights of way, waste disposal systems (e.g., septic tanks), water systems and water quality (e.g., checking wells) to name a few. Find out in advance what is included and excluded. Inspections such as septic, water and well, mould, wood destroying insects (WDI), or radon tests may need to be completed by inspectors specifically qualified in these areas.

3. Is an Inspection Needed for a Newly Constructed Home?

It's new so what could be wrong? Is it wise to spend the time and money to have a new home inspected? Most new homes allow a pre-delivery inspection (PDI) a day or two prior to closing. During the inspection you would walk around the home with an employee of the builder viewing the home with the intention of reporting any flaws, mistakes, or deficiencies, usually noted on a PDI report. If repairs are required, after closing, many if not all are covered by the builder's warranty within the first six months to one year. However, it is very important that you properly report these deficiencies in a timely manner, otherwise they may not be covered. You will need to decide if you feel more comfortable having a home inspector accompany you during the pre-delivery inspection.

10

The Role of Your Lawyer

s a general rule of thumb, it is always a good idea to have a lawyer review and advise you on any contract or legal transaction. A lawyer is a valuable part of your home-buying team. Even though it is legal to buy and sell property yourself, it is prudent to meet with and select a lawyer early in your home-buying process.

From a practical perspective, sometimes timing doesn't enable your lawyer to review your offer prior to presenting it to the seller. Some agreements of purchase and sale are drafted, presented to the seller, and negotiated in the evening or on weekends when it may be difficult to contact a lawyer (in this case, remember the condition about lawyer approval from Chapter 8).

The agreement of purchase and sale and the mortgage documents are very important contracts in the home-buying process. These documents, when signed, are legal and binding contracts. Buyers often inquire whether they should have an agreement of purchase and sale reviewed by a lawyer prior to signing it. In a perfect world the answer is "yes." These documents are filled with legal terms and language with which you are probably not familiar. A lawyer will read through and advise you on all the legalese contained in the documents to make sure that your rights and interests are protected and that you understand your responsibilities and liabilities.

Usually the resale agreement of purchase and sale is completed by the buyer's real estate professional. It is recommended that you forward your agreement of purchase and sale to your lawyer for review and comments prior to signing. This way you can be assured that the appropriate and legal wording of clauses to protect your interest has been addressed.

Some buyers may be concerned that a lawyer will charge them to review the contract in advance, and they are not sure they will even be able to successfully negotiate the agreement. Some lawyers may charge to review the contract, while others include reviews in their rate to complete the transaction. Take the appropriate precautions to protect yourself. Work out a plan of action with your legal professional in advance. Some buyers discuss clauses and conditions with their lawyer in advance of finding a home and other buyers may insert a condition in their offer that is conditional on legal review and approval. Some lawyers make themselves available evenings or weekends via email, faxes, and smart phones — communication is easier than ever these days.

Many residential resale agreements of purchase and sale are on pre-printed forms from the local real estate board or provincial real estate association. Any additional clauses are added in the blank spots or on a separate schedule.

New home agreements of purchase and sale may be different from resale agreements. They can be quite lengthy, complicated, and may include substantial additional costs that the builder is passing on to the buyer. Normally, the new home builder provides the agreement of purchase and sale which has been drafted by the builder's lawyer with the builder's best interests in mind. Additionally, you have no representation by the builder's salesperson who may or may not be licensed real estate professionals as it may not (depending on the province) be a requirement when employed by a new home builder. The builder's salesperson does not have the same fiduciary duties or obligations a buyer's agent would.

In some provinces, such as Ontario, with new condominium purchases, there is a ten-day *cooling off* period, which means you can change your mind within ten days and void the deal. Occasionally, salespeople at new condominium sales sites will ask you to sign an agreement of purchase and sale right away using the tradeoff that there is the ten-day cooling off period. Check the rules in your province.

It is wise to err on the cautious side and, at the very least, insert that condition into the agreement stating that the sale is conditional upon your lawyer's review and approval. Even better, it is preferred that you ask the builder's salesperson for a copy of the agreement which you can take to your lawyer for review prior to signing; this way you are made aware of the details and legalese involved with the agreement.

You may find that your lawyer suggests certain clauses be modified or eliminated. Sometimes there are substantial additional charges or other obligations and liabilities in the fine print of the builder's agreement. You will want to have the charges capped or have an upper ceiling stated. This is very important especially with properties that are not yet built. So many things can occur, and you want to protect yourself and understand everything.

Since a lawyer will become an integral part of your buying process, why not find a lawyer prior to purchasing a property? With respect to a new construction agreement of purchase and sale, normally due to the length of the agreement and schedules and the amount of time it takes for the lawyer to review, there may be an additional fee. Ask the lawyer for a breakdown of the fees in advance.

Note: Notaries in Québec are not the same as notaries in the rest of Canada. For details about Québec notary services refer to www.cdnq.org.

1. How to Find the Right Lawyer

Many first-time buyers have never had to utilize the services of a lawyer of any kind until they want to buy homes, so how do people find and select the right lawyer for their real estate purchase? Most home buyers find their lawyer by a referral from friends, family, or associates. Lawyers have a license to practice law, so consider selecting a lawyer that specifically practices real estate law because he or she is trained and experienced with the ins and outs of real estate issues.

Don't be afraid to ask questions when you are speaking with a lawyer. Inquire about his or her real estate experience. Find out if he or she has experience dealing with new construction purchase and sale contracts (if appropriate). Ask how his or her fees are broken down and ask for an estimate of disbursements. Keep in mind that the fee will vary depending on the amount of work he or she will do and the overall complexity of the transaction.

Legal costs are sometimes broken into two separate parts:

- **Lawyer's fee:** Ask if this includes the work involved with a mortgage.

- **Disbursements:** These are out-of-pocket expenses. Most lawyers will quote you a small range for the likely costs of disbursements.

You want a quote, in total of what the anticipated legal bill will be for everything (including the mortgage). If possible, obtain the quote in writing.

Ask if the lawyer is available on weekends and evenings (just in case you are ready to sign an agreement of purchase and sale at that time) and if so, how you can contact him or her.

Legal fees will vary depending on the lawyer; consider getting an estimate. Be careful about selecting a lawyer solely on price; remember, experience is an asset and real estate law is a specialty. When a lawyer graduates, he or she has a licence to practice law. Laws change, so you want a lawyer who is up to date on real estate changes and procedures that could apply to your transaction. If there is ever an issue with your closing, you want a lawyer who is knowledgeable and experienced handling the situation. There is no substitute for knowledge and experience. You also want someone you feel comfortable with who is approachable and available. Ideally, you want an experienced real estate lawyer, who charges a reasonable and fair price, with a good reputation. Do your homework, ask around, check references, and compare.

2. What Is the Lawyer's Role When Closing Your Deal?

Once you have a signed and accepted agreement of purchase and sale (which hopefully was reviewed and approved by your lawyer prior to becoming a firm and binding transaction), your lawyer will begin the legal closing process. You should ensure that your lawyer gets a copy of the agreement as soon as possible, and before the date known as the requisition date (or title search date). This is a date in the contract, which is the deadline for your lawyer to object to any problems found with the title.

Your lawyer has a lot of work to do now. One of his or her most important duties is to certify that you have valid title. Processes and searches may vary depending on the province; the following is an example of what normally occurs in Ontario.

The lawyer will search to ensure there are no liens or claims registered against the property and that it is not subject to encroachments, easements, encumbrances, and mortgages that may not be identified in the agreement. He or she will also check the conveyance of the property with adjoining lands. Your lawyer will check that the named seller on the agreement is the actual owner of the property. These searches are done prior to the requisition (title search) date and once again on the closing date.

The lawyer will also check with the municipality for any property taxes owed on the home and may request a property tax certificate to confirm that current and past years' taxes are paid. This will be itemized on the statement of adjustments that the lawyer will provide on closing. Any arrears or overpayments will be adjusted at that time. Letters will be sent to building, zoning, utilities, and planning departments to confirm that there are no arrears for water, hydro/electricity, or gas and that there are no sales contracts, easements, liens, encumbrances, and bylaws that could cause problems.

If you are closing on a new home, the lawyer will check that the final inspection has been completed. Information regarding any outstanding work orders, confirmation of subdivision, and any other agreements may also be requested.

Your lawyer will check to ensure there is nothing about the seller or prior owners that may affect your title. This includes but isn't limited to judgments. Occasionally, when a match is found it is someone with a similar name which means your lawyer will have to obtain information and statutory declarations that the owner is not the person concerned.

If you have a mortgage, your lawyer will also have to search for executions against you, the buyer, as the lawyer must also ensure that the lender is protected. Once again, if a match is found and it is not you but someone with a similar name, your lawyer will have to obtain evidence that it is not you, which may cost you additional legal fees or disbursements.

Once all the searches are completed prior to the requisition date, your lawyer will send a letter to the seller's lawyer outlining any problems and request that they be remedied on or before the closing. If the problems cannot be corrected, your lawyer will advise you of your options. Your lawyer will also send a few documents that the sellers will need to sign such as warranties, bill of sale, and other declarations.

You will want proof of the seller's residency to confirm whether the seller is a foreigner as there may be a withholding requirement. When foreigners sell real estate they are required to obtain a clearance certificate from Canada Revenue Agency (CRA). The purpose of the certificate is to ensure that any and all tax that is owed to CRA is collected. The clearance certificate can take six to ten weeks to obtain. If the closing date occurs prior to receipt of the certificate, your lawyer will withhold 25 percent of the sale price until the certificate is issued; otherwise, you can be liable to CRA for the foreigner's unpaid tax. Check with your lawyer regarding the documentation and proof of the seller's residency status to ensure that you are protected.

The mortgage lender will forward a mortgage package to your lawyer for closing which will include instructions and conditions for the mortgage. (Make sure the lender knows your lawyer's name and contact information.) Your lawyer will prepare the paperwork for the mortgage and must ensure that the conditions of the mortgage commitment are met. Your lawyer will need to certify title of the property to the lender as well as you, the buyer. In many cases, lenders require that a title insurance policy covering their interest is provided and paid for by the buyer. Make sure you discuss this with your lawyer.

The lender will provide your lawyer with a mortgage commitment letter which you will need to sign. It is a good idea to review the commitment letter with your lawyer and mortgage professional so that you understand all the costs, terms, and conditions prior to signing it.

Your lawyer will discuss how you wish title to be taken. If you are planning to take title in your name, usually this is done either as joint tenants or tenants in common. Joint tenancy has rights of survivorship. For example, assuming there are two owners, when one joint tenant (owner) dies the entire property belongs to the surviving joint tenant. Only the last person left can give the property to someone else. This is often used by married couples so if one spouse dies, the property automatically goes to the survivor without having to go through probate. Tenants in common is different; each person owns a half, third, fourth, or some other portion that belongs to the individual person, in equal or unequal shares. In this type of ownership arrangement each owner can leave his or her share to someone in his or her will, or even sell his or her share. Each ownership type has different considerations so make sure that your lawyer explains all of your options, which may vary depending on the province and your situation. (Couples should discuss property rights as they relate to marriage and common-law relationships in the province or territory of purchase.) Your lawyer will also review and verify the deed, transfer, certificate of title (i.e., the document that transfers ownership [title] of the property from the seller to the buyer), the statement of adjustments, and other closing information that is sent by the seller's lawyer.

Prior to your closing date (ideally as soon as possible after you have an accepted agreement of purchase and sale) you will need to contact your insurance agent to arrange homeowner's insurance to begin on your closing day. This is a good idea regardless of whether you have a mortgage (note that it is mandatory if you have a mortgage). You will provide the insurance company with your lawyer's and lender's name and contact information as the lender's name will be stated on your insurance policy. Usually the insurance company will send your lawyer a binder confirming insurance is in place beginning on the closing date, and that the lender's name is noted. It is important to make sure that your insurance company sends this information to your lawyer in advance; otherwise, your closing may be delayed. The bottom line is the lender will not generally advance funds until it has proof that an appropriate insurance policy is in place effective on the day of closing.

Sometimes a property survey is available and included with purchase. It is always beneficial to have this document and you should specifically ask for it in your agreement of purchase and sale (excluding condominium and co-op properties). Check the survey to make sure all boundaries are defined, and all buildings and improvements are located within boundary lines and comply with zoning and setback requirements. Surveys show the dimensions of the property as well as the easements. Lenders will usually ask for a survey (if available) and may (depending on the lender and the province) request a title insurance policy prior to advancing funds. Issues can arise if the property has had an addition or a pool added since the last survey as it will not be shown on the plan of survey. This may necessitate getting it updated, obtaining a new survey, and/or getting title insurance. If this occurs, discuss with your lawyer. If time is a factor, getting a new survey will take longer than obtaining a title policy.

When possible, it is still prudent to obtain a survey from the seller; consider making your offer conditional on your satisfaction with the survey contents. If you plan on building a deck, adding an addition, or installing a pool, you will likely need the survey in order to obtain a permit. Also, buyers in the future (if you sell at some point) may ask for a survey so this may alleviate any future negotiations on this item.

3. Closing Costs

Closing is the day that you take legal possession of your home. Money and keys are exchanged and documents are registered. The final signing of all documents usually occurs at the lawyer or notary's office on the closing day (or a day or two before). At this meeting you will bring a certified cheque to cover any balance of the down payment that may be owed along with closing costs. You will be advised in advance how much is due at the meeting.

In addition to the purchase price of the home, there are other expenses for which you need to budget. Closing costs are expenses that you pay when you purchase a home, usually before you move in. Possible closing costs may include:

- **Appraisal fee:** As previously discussed, your lender will lend a percentage of the home's purchase price or the market value of the home — whichever is lower. To determine the market value, the lender will hire an appraiser to confirm the value. Often you are required to pay for the appraisal — check with your lender or mortgage broker.

- **Lender's application fee:** Some lenders will charge an application fee to process your mortgage and some will waive this fee. Confirm with your lender or mortgage broker.

- **Legal or notary fees:** Typically these fees are billed as legal fees and disbursements (i.e., out-of-pocket expenses).

- **Mortgage broker fee:** Find out in advance if your mortgage broker charges you a separate fee. Often this is not the case because he or she is paid by the lender. Confirm this with your mortgage professional.

- **Real estate professional fee:** Determine in advance the amount and how your real estate professional is paid. Often he or she is paid by the company that has listed the property; however, some buyer agency contracts may differ or special circumstances may arise, and you may owe the real estate professional a commission.

- **Title insurance premium:** Normally your lawyer arranges a title insurance policy which you usually pay for (unless otherwise stated in your agreement; ask if unsure).

- **Property insurance premium:** You will need to arrange for property insurance coverage to begin on closing that covers fire and usually third-party liability. This is normally billed to you directly from the insurance company.

- **Mortgage life or term insurance:** Some buyers consider purchasing mortgage life or term insurance. Find out from the insurer how and when you are required to pay the premium.

- **Land survey:** You may or may not be required to obtain a new survey — check with your real estate professional and lender. Often an existing survey is available and is sufficient.

- **Home inspection, water tests, septic tests, well tests, WETT certification, and other home related expenses:** Often these are paid for prior to closing; however, it is a good idea to include these costs in your budget.

- **Prepaid property taxes:** There may be an adjustment included on your final statement of adjustments if the seller has prepaid the property tax. You will have to reimburse the seller for any amount he or she overpaid.

- **Other miscellaneous costs:** There may be adjustments for utilities (e.g., heating, oil). You may be required to fill an oil tank and pay sales tax on an insurance premium.

- **Estoppel or status certificate:** This is a document that provides information on condominium properties.

- **Goods and Services Tax (GST) or Harmonized Sales Tax (HST):** GST is a value added tax. HST is a combination of GST and PST that some provinces use. Provinces and territories have different tax and different goods and services which are taxed. GST or HST may be due on the real estate commissions, and may also be charged on an appraisal, survey, and other real estate related services. Ensure that you are aware of the taxes relative to your provincial laws as well as the type and use of the property. Check to ensure that there is no additional GST or HST added to the purchase price that you are responsible for and that you are aware in advance of all taxes prior to committing to a purchase.

Check with your accountant or lawyer and province on whether you may be eligible for a tax rebate when you purchase new construction or an extensively renovated home.

- **Land transfer tax:** This is a tax that in most provinces is charged just because you bought a home. All provinces have a form of land transfer tax except Alberta and Saskatchewan, which charge a smaller transfer fee. The amount of land transfer tax in the other provinces depends on the value of the home. Ontario, British Columbia and Prince Edward Island, as well as the city of Toronto itself have land transfer tax rebates for first-time buyers.

- **Other expenses:** Other expenses may include moving or storage costs, redirecting mail, utility hook-up fees, and buying new appliances.

It is important to understand that processes, expenses, and laws vary depending on the province or territory. For example, in some provinces it may be common for a lawyer to assist a buyer with the process of closing and conveying the transfer of title; in other provinces it may be common for buyers to work with a notary or other type of professional. Documentation and wording, searches, fees, requirements, and laws differ depending on the province. Also, note that laws can and do change. The information covered in this chapter relates to what usually occurs in the province of Ontario. It is recommended that you consult with a lawyer in the province you purchase to confirm the laws, processes, and requirements related to that specific province.

3.1 Ontario land transfer tax

When you purchase land or an interest in land in Ontario, you will be paying on closing a tax known as the land transfer tax. Land includes existing buildings, buildings to be constructed, and fixtures. It is a mathematical calculation based on the purchase price as follows:

- 0.5 percent on amounts up to and including the first $55,000, plus

- 1 percent of the amount exceeding $55,000 to and including $250,000, plus

- 1.5 percent of the amount exceeding $250,000, plus

- 2 percent of the amount exceeding $400,000 where the land contains one and not more than two single-family residences.

If you purchase a home in the city of Toronto, you will also pay, in addition to the provincial land transfer tax, a Municipal Land Transfer Tax (MLTT). The land transfer tax is payable on registration and transfer of title. The MLTT is charged on a graduated basis; for property containing one, but not more than two single-family residences the MLTT rates are as follows:

- Up to and including $55,000.00: the rate is 0.5 percent

- $55,000.01 to $400,000.00: the rate is 1 percent

- More than $400,000.00: the rate is 2 percent

For additional information go to www.ontario.ca.

3.2 British Columbia property transfer tax

British Columbia home buyers pay what is called Property Transfer Tax. It is a land registration tax and is paid to the Land Title Office to register changes to a certificate of title. It is payable on the fair market value of the property being transferred. Fair market value is defined as the price that a willing buyer and willing seller would pay on the open market — often it is the purchase price of the property. The amount of tax is based on the fair market value of the property being transferred, and is calculated as follows:

- 1 percent on the first $200,000 of the fair market value of the property, plus

- 2 percent on the fair market value of more than $200,000.

Transactions are taxable at fair market value regardless of the purchase price; a gift of property still requires a Property Transfer Tax to be paid, as does any fee simple transfers.

For additional information go to www.rev.gov.bc.ca.

3.3 Prince Edward Island first-time buyer land transfer tax

Prince Edward Island's first-time buyer land transfer tax is calculated as follows:

- 1 percent of the greater of purchase price or assessed value of the property. There is no transfer tax on property valued at less than $30,000.

For additional information go to www.gov.pe.ca.

3.4 Alberta and Saskatchewan land transfer fees

Alberta and Saskatchewan do not have a land transfer tax; however, both charge a form of title transfer fees.

3.5 Manitoba land transfer tax

Land transfer tax is payable in Manitoba, along with a registration fee upon registration of transfer of title. The tax is calculated based on the fair market value of real estate on the day of registration and calculated as follows:

- On the first $30,000: the rate is $0
- $30,001 to $90,000: the rate is 0.5 percent
- $90,001 to $150,000: the rate is 1.0 percent
- $150,001 to $200,000: the rate is 1.5 percent
- Excess of $200,000: the rate is 2.0 percent

For additional information go to www.manitoba.ca.

3.6 Québec land transfer tax

Québec land transfer tax is calculated as follows:

- First $50,000: the rate is 0.5 percent
- $50,001 to $250,000: the rate is 1.0 percent
- More than $250,000: the rate is 1.5 percent

For additional information go to www.gouv.qc.ca.

3.7 New Brunswick real property transfer tax

The land transfer tax is 0.25 percent of the assessed value of the property. As an example, on a purchase of a home for $200,000, the tax payable is $500.

For additional information go to www.gnb.ca.

3.8 Nova Scotia land transfer tax

Land transfer rates vary depending on whether the home is located in the Halifax area or outside the Halifax area. For homes in the Halifax area, the land transfer tax is 1.5 percent of the purchase price of the home. For homes outside the Halifax area, refer to the Nova Scotia land transfer tax tables.

For additional information go to www.gov.ns.ca.

3.9 Newfoundland registration of deeds

Newfoundland and Labrador land transfer tax is payable on the property value and mortgage amounts calculated as follows:

- Less than $500 for a flat fee of $100

- More than $500 — $100 + 0.4 percent of the mortgage amount is charged

For additional information go to www.gs.gov.nl.ca.

3.10 Northwest Territories land transfer tax

The Northwest Territories' land transfer tax is calculated as a percentage of the property value and mortgage amount:

- $1.50 for every $1,000 or part thereof of property value (minimum $100 charge)

- $1.00 for every $1,000 or part thereof of property value (for part of property value greater than $1,000,000)

- $1.00 for every $5,000 or part thereof of mortgage amount (minimum $80 charge)

For additional information go to www.gov.nt.ca.

3.11 Yukon Territory land title

The Yukon Territory fee is payable on registration of transfer and calculated as follows:

- First $1,000 is $6.00

- $1,000 to $3,000 is $7.50

- $3,000 to $5,000 is $10.50

- Each $1,000 or portion thereof that is more than $5,000 to $10,000 is a rate of $1.50

- Each $1,000 or portion thereof that is more than $10,000 to $25,000 is a rate of $0.75

- Each $1,000 or portion therefore that is more than $25,000 is a rate of $0.25

For additional information go to www.justice.gov.yk.ca.

3.12 Nunavut

Most properties come with land leases (up to 30 years and renewable). Therefore, normally there is no "land transfer." There is a land lease registration fee of a maximum $400. Additionally there is a 1 percent fee for mortgages (for example, a $100,000 mortgage has a $1,000 registration fee).

For additional information go to www.justice.gov.nu.ca.

4. Closing Tasks

Prior to closing there are a few items that you will want to complete including the following (use Worksheet 4 to keep track):

- Contact utility companies such as hydro/electricity, water, and gas to set up your accounts.

- Contact telephone, cable or satellite TV, Internet, and alarm monitoring companies to set up accounts and arrange for services to your home.

- Complete an address change card either at your local post office or online at www.canadapost.ca.

- Change your address on your driver's licence and provincial health card, and with any other relevant provincial health and licensing body.

- Notify your landlord of your moving date if you are currently renting.

- Arrange for a truck, moving company, or friends and family to help with your move. Obtain quotes and compare prices for rentals and movers — often a midweek or mid-month move is less expensive.

Worksheet 4
Closing Tasks

_____ Contact utility companies to set up accounts in your name:
    _____ Gas
    _____ Hydro
    _____ Water and sewage

_____ Contact other services to set up accounts in your name:
    _____ Telephone provider
    _____ Cable or satellite TV provider
    _____ Internet provider
    _____ Alarm-monitoring company

_____ Change of address
    _____ Post office
    _____ Banks
    _____ Credit cards
    _____ Other: _____
    _____ Other: _____

_____ Driver's licence and insurance

_____ Provincial health care

_____ Landlord (give notice)

_____ Movers (book truck and movers)

_____ Register children at new school

_____ Homeowners' insurance (ensure binder of policy sent to lawyer and lender)

_____ Other: _____

_____ Other: _____

_____ Other: _____

- Double check that your home insurer has sent confirmation to your lawyer and lender for your home insurance policy.

On closing, your lender will advance the mortgage money to your lawyer or notary. You will also be paying the remaining closing costs. This total will be provided to you, usually the day before by your lawyer or notary. Your lawyer or notary will pay the seller (or the seller's lawyer or notary), register the deed and any relevant documents, and give you the deed and keys to your home.

5. Will and Powers of Attorney

Once you are a homeowner you should consider having a will prepared. You may want to discuss the preparation of a will with your lawyer during your first meeting. A will takes effect when you die; should you pass away without a will, the distribution of your assets can be somewhat complicated (and the people you want to receive your property may not be the ones who get it), and it can involve additional legal fees to probate your estate. If you want to have a say about who is to receive what you possess, you need to prepare a will. See *Write Your Legal Will in 3 Easy Steps*, also published by Self-Counsel Press, for a simple, step-by-step will. You may wish to seek legal advice about this important document.

If you were to become incapacitated, a power of attorney document can help. There are powers of attorney for property and health care. A power of attorney for property allows the person you select to control your assets. This ensures that if you are not able to manage your affairs, the person you choose can manage them. A health-care power of attorney allows a health-care professional to speak with whomever you choose who can give direction about your health if you cannot give instructions about your care. For more information, Self-Counsel Press also publishes *Power of Attorney Kit*.

It is recommended that you discuss with your lawyer the preparation of a will along with powers of attorney to ensure your affairs are handled the way you would want, should the unforeseen happen.

11

Title Insurance

Title insurance is an insurance policy that is obtained on the closing or completion date of a real estate transaction; this is the date when title is transferred. The purpose of title insurance is to protect the purchaser (new owner), or the lender, or both against certain outlined items known as *perils* related to the quality of the title. Perils are defined in the title policy, they are a specific risk or loss covered by the insurance policy. Examples of perils that may be covered include prior undischarged mortgages, defects shown on a survey, a document that is not properly signed, and forgery and fraud. It is a one-time policy that lasts the entire time you own the property.

The use of title insurance in Canada is relatively new, although it has been used in the United States for many years. In Canada, title insurance initially became popular when a survey wasn't available because it would insure against survey defects that may be found if a survey was obtained. Purchasing title insurance was usually quicker and helped with quick closings.

The use and popularity of title insurance has grown in recent years. Home ownership for most people is likened to financial security. This security is increasingly at risk with title fraud and forgery.

Keep in mind that title insurance protects against more than defects that may be revealed in a survey.

Usually when closing a real estate transaction, lawyers do title searches in order to provide their opinion on the title, which in essence describes who has the rights of ownership to the property. The lawyers, through their various searches, review the records to determine if the seller listed on the agreement actually owns the property and has the right and ability to sell the property as well as verify that there are no issues or problems with title. The goal is for the buyer to acquire clear title to the property so that he or she may sell the property in the future.

In Ontario, in addition to doing title searches, the lawyer also conducts other searches such as checking with the building department to determine if the location of the home on the property complies with setback requirements, and checks with various government bodies to ensure the property complies with bylaws. The lawyer also reviews the records for utilities and property tax to ensure they are current. Once all the searches and verifications are complete, the lawyers provide their opinion or certification on title. (The types of searches may vary depending on the province.) Both the buyer and the lender rely on the lawyer's certification of title to advance the funds and close on the transaction.

Most of the time this all works fine; but once in a while, however rare, the certification is wrong. What if the records that were searched contained errors? If an error is discovered after the closing, the lawyer is covered by his or her own insurance; but what about the buyer and the lender?

Mistakes and inaccuracies can occur with records; this could prove to be a very time-consuming and costly experience for the buyer to remedy. Additionally, if no error is made, a neighbour could later complain that an addition to the home or garage is too close to his or her property, for example. As the owner, you would have to deal with this issue.

It is difficult to predict what can go wrong and unknown issues and defects can come up that can be financially and emotionally draining. Despite your lawyer's searches and due diligence, other issues can occur such as fraud and forgery.

1. Title Insurance and How It Protects the Buyer

Title insurance protects the buyer and lender with a guarantee from the insurer. The buyer and the lender are covered against title defects, survey defects (e.g., encroachments, infractions of bylaws), and fraud and forgery as listed in the policy. The title insurer assumes the risks.

Usually the buyer pays a one-time fee to the insurer. Insurance companies offer policies for owners and policies for lenders — rates may vary. For the premium paid to the insurer, the home buyer gets protection for as long as he or she owns the home. The title insurance policy is not *ported* or taken to a new home should the buyer sell his or her home and purchase another home. The buyer would obtain a new title policy for another home purchase and closing. In some provinces, lenders make it mandatory that there is a lender's title policy prior to funding the transaction.

Title insurance does not eliminate the role of a lawyer; the buyer's lawyer still performs the title searches and the insurer analyzes the risk. Additionally, title insurance does not replace the lawyer doing title searches and providing a certification of title; rather it adds an element of protection. (You can also ask the seller to supply an up-to-date survey of the property to review with your lawyer as it may show potential defects, encroachments, easements, or boundaries.) The title is insured on the closing date and the insurance provides coverage or protection against title defects as outlined in the policy. Simply put, title insurance enhances the lawyer's work.

Let's consider fraud and forgery. What if a mortgage was discharged fraudulently or documents were forged? Lawyers are not responsible for this and this could be difficult if not impossible to find out. How can this happen you ask?

Consider this: A tenant poses as a seller. What if the seller's real estate professional or lawyer does not know the seller personally and does not ask for photo identification? (Note that real estate professionals should obtain photo ID; in some provinces this is mandatory.) What if a false ID is used? Given that the tenant (posing as the seller) lives in the home and may provide the deed and mortgage (which are relatively easy to obtain), who would know that the occupant (tenant) is not the seller? You purchase, close, and move into the property; at some point in the future, the real owner stops by and you both find out what has occurred. Imagine the disaster if you did not have title insurance that covered this type of fraud?

Today it is common practice for lawyers to register documents (i.e., deeds, mortgages, discharge of mortgages) through an online password-protected interface. However, with the rise in online hacking, it is possible that a would-be perpetrator could get into the land registry system and randomly select your property for fraud or forgery. The risk may be low, but anything is possible. Confirm that your title policy includes coverage for an illegal sale of the property as well as fraud and forgery.

Title insurance is important when purchasing a condo. For example, in Ontario, often as part of a condominium transaction, the buyer requests what is known as a *status certificate* of the condominium corporation (may also be referred to as an *estoppel certificate*). This includes a breakdown of the condominium corporation's finances — including budgets, reserves, and planned expenditures. If there are not enough funds in the reserve fund to cover future planned repairs and improvements, the cost of the repairs could be charged back to the individual unit owners. This is known as a *special assessment*. If the status certificate states there are no special assessments planned, and then shortly after closing and moving into the condominium you receive a bill for a special assessment, this may be covered by your title insurance policy. These are just a few examples of what a title insurance policy may cover — there may be more.

Prior to title insurance, recovery from loss or damage due to title problems was dependent on being able to make a successful claim against someone else. This is not only time consuming and emotionally draining, it can also be expensive. If you have title insurance, you are likely covered. Title insurance compensates you against the loss on a no-fault basis. It is imperative that you check with the insurer and your lawyer about what is covered in your title policy.

With quick closings it can be difficult, if not impossible, to get all the letters and certificates related to searches completed on time — especially if there appears to be a problem. Once again, check with the insurer and your lawyer to determine exactly what is covered — and read the fine print.

As previously explained, title insurance can assist with property survey issues. Many lenders require a new or up-to-date survey of the property prior to advancing funds. Often, especially in older, established communities, a survey is not available. Or, if the subject property has had additions such as a pool, deck, or sunroom, it may not be shown on the existing survey. Obtaining a new or up-to-date survey can be costly and time consuming and, in some cases, could delay a closing. Title insurance policies for the lender protect the lender from any property defect that it would have found in a current survey, and can alleviate the need for a new survey.

Having said this, a buyer will still require a survey if he or she plans to do an addition or add a pool in the future because the city or municipality will normally request this before issuing a building permit. Should you sell the property at some point in the future, the future buyer may also ask for a survey, so try to get one from the seller.

Title insurance assumes the liability for any title defects, and problems are dealt with through a claim rather than time-consuming and expensive litigation.

The use of title insurance in Canada is growing rapidly. Numerous lawyers embrace and recommend title insurance to their clients. A recent amendment in Ontario requires that a lawyer must advise his or her clients that they have a choice between the lawyer's opinion on title and title insurance. In other words, Ontario lawyers are obligated to make you aware of title insurance.

2. Title Insurance and What It Doesn't Cover

There are a few things that aren't covered by your title insurance. Your lawyer should review what is and what is not included with your policy. Exceptions to coverage include:

- Value of the home. The title insurance is not an appraisal so the value of the home is not insured.

- Defects that do not cause a loss to the buyer.

- Defects known to the owner but not disclosed to insurer prior to closing, and the buyer agreed to the defects.

- Some environmental hazards such as soil contamination.

- Government expropriation rights. Normally, in this case, the government would compensate the buyer.

Laws may vary province to province. For example, in one province, title insurance may not guarantee the property can be resold without obtaining a real property report and zoning compliance certificate, or a new title insurance policy at that time. When you originally purchase a property, if you accept the property on the basis of the title insurance policy, and if you decide to sell the property at some point in the future, you may be required to provide to the buyer a new real property report — and it may be at your cost. These expenses may be avoided if, when you purchased the property you or your lawyer insisted that the seller provide a survey or real property report and zoning compliance certificate, which you would keep in your possession and deliver to a future buyer when you sell your home.

Without trying to sound like a broken record, it is recommended that you check with your lawyer and insurer to find out what is covered and what is not covered. Laws may vary depending on the province, and laws can and do change. The onus is on you to make a prudent and informed decision. There may be a difference between what is covered in an owner's policy versus a lender's policy. If there is a mortgage on the property, there will likely be two separate policies: one for the owner and one for the lender.

3. How Do You Choose a Title Insurance Company?

Title insurance coverage is similar with most of the insurance companies. Normally your lawyer will review with you the various choices of insurance companies — your lawyer may even have one or two that he or she prefers. Do your homework and investigate the company. Most companies have a website. Ask about the company's claims process, what is covered, and how you can contact the company.

Keep in mind, title insurance is an insurance product. It is important to review your policy and ask questions if in doubt. Understand your coverage.

The following title insurance companies operate in Canada:

- First Canadian Title (FCT): www.firstcanadiantitle.com
- Stewart Title Guaranty Company: www.stewart.ca
- Chicago Title Canada: www.ctic.com
- TitlePLUS: www.lawpro.ca
- Traveler's Canada: www.travelerscanada.ca

Visit their websites for more information regarding costs, coverage, and benefits.

4. What Does Title Insurance Cost?

Premiums vary between companies. The type of property you are buying has different risks and as such, different premiums. In general, condominiums are the lowest priced, then new homes, and lastly resale homes. Pricing varies from $175 to $1,000 depending on the type of home assuming a purchase price of $500,000 or less. Obviously homes in excess of $500,000 will likely cost more for title insurance. Check with your lawyer for an accurate quote for title insurance.

5. How Do I Obtain a Title Policy?

Title insurance coverage may vary depending on the province. In Ontario, where it is mandatory that your lawyer offer you a title insurance policy, you would have your lawyer arrange for it as part of the closing process. If you have a mortgage in Ontario, most, if not all lenders in Ontario will require a title insurance policy. Not all provinces have the same rules regarding title insurance. Check with your lawyer for the laws in your province.

Discuss this with your lawyer and real estate professional, and investigate the option of obtaining a title policy and its coverage. Don't assume that all provinces have the same rules regarding the availability, coverage, and price of title insurance. Although the acceptance and growth of title insurance has been very strong in general, be sure to check with your lawyer, as well as the title company for information specific to your province, specific property, and other needs.

12

Home and Property Insurance

1. Property and Contents Insurance

Prior to closing your real estate transaction, you will want to get property insurance to protect the building, the contents inside, and to cover third-party liability. Obviously, with such a large investment you want to be protected. If you are getting a mortgage, the lender will make obtaining property insurance coverage mandatory by the closing date or it will not advance funds for the closing. You will be required to name your lender in your policy as the lender will want to protect its interest. Ongoing coverage is normally a condition of the mortgage. For these reasons it is prudent to apply and acquire an insurance policy as soon as possible after an agreement of purchase and sale is accepted.

The insurance representative will usually ask questions about the home such as the following:

- Type of home
- Age of the home
- Type of heating, and if oil, the age of the oil tank and its certification
- Type of roof (e.g., shingle, tile, steel) and age of roof

- Type of wiring (e.g., copper or aluminum)
- Type of construction (e.g., brick, wood frame, cinder block)
- Proximity to fire hydrant and possibly even the proximity to a fire station
- Whether or not there is a security alarm
- Square footage of the home

Some insurers visit the home to visually inspect the interior and exterior.

The insurance company considers many factors when determining what type of policy to sell, how much the policy will cost, and whether it is willing to insure your home. There are a few different types of insurance policies and coverage. Since coverage varies, it is important that you are aware of what is covered in your particular policy. You will want to consider the following questions:

- Does the policy include replacement value coverage?
- Are you covered for sewer backup?
- What is the personal liability limit?
- What is the personal property (i.e., contents) coverage value?

Usually home insurance policies have limits on theft coverage for jewellery, furs, and money; normally you can purchase additional coverage if required. Homeowners' policies often exclude certain perils so don't wait until a loss occurs to find out what your policy does or does not cover. You may be able to purchase optional coverage known as *endorsements* to protect against some of the excluded perils. It is very important to ask your insurance representative for details of what is included and not included. Ask for specific details and understand value limitations.

Sometimes discounts may be available for homeowners with sprinkler systems, monitored burglar and fire alarms that report to a central service, and fire extinguishers. Discounts may also be available if you have other policies, such as vehicle insurance or life insurance with the same insurance company. The amount of the deductible can also affect the price; usually the higher the deductible, the lower the premium.

Buyers of condominiums will want coverage to insure for their personal belongings (i.e., contents), liability, and structural improvements inside the unit. Normally the condominium corporation has a separate policy to cover damages as well as liability in the common areas of the building such as roof, parking, lobby, and swimming pool. Take the time to find out what the condominium corporations' policy insures specifically; for example, does the policy insure the bare walls, ceiling, and floor of your unit? Are you responsible for cabinets, wiring, plumbing, and fixtures? Knowing this will give you the information needed to review, with the insurance representative, the coverage options available to ensure you have proper and adequate insurance coverage.

There are a number of home issues that can create a problem when applying for coverage including the following:

- Sixty-amp electrical service may not be enough for the size of the home and may require updating

- Aluminum wiring or knob and tube wiring may need to be retrofitted or changed

- Wood-burning appliances may require Wood Energy Technology Transfer (WETT) certification

- Oil tanks may need certification

- Mould may be a problem

- Roof may need replacing, especially if it is older than 20 years

- Heritage or century homes may need special care because of galvanized pipes, type of heating, and wiring

- Location of home could be a concern relative to areas prone to natural disasters such as flooding, forest fires, and other extreme weather conditions

Buyers should put home insurance at the top of their to-do list. Consider obtaining written confirmation of insurance coverage as a contingency in the agreement, especially if you are purchasing a home that may present any insurance coverage challenges.

If you plan to rent out any portion of the home (assuming it is appropriate and legal), you will need to discuss this with the insurance company or insurance agent. There may be restrictions on theft and damage by the tenants. Find out in advance all the inclusions and exclusions in the policy.

Home insurance is an important decision. Invest the time to learn about the insurance products, features, and options that are available. Speak with experienced and trained insurance professionals who will educate you. If in doubt, ask questions, or perhaps speak with your lawyer should you want any clarification of the legal contents of a policy. Ensure that you understand what your policy includes and excludes, and what limitations it may have.

2. Mortgage Insurance

In addition to property and title insurance, there are a number of life and mortgage insurance options available. It goes without saying that your home is likely your single largest investment, so peace of mind can be a good thing.

Although we all hope to live long, healthy, and happy lives, sometimes things happen. If you were to pass away and there was a mortgage on your home to pay, what would happen? Who would pay it? How would this affect your family?

Spend time investigating your options. There are a number of different types of policies, each with their own features and costs.

Mortgage life insurance is offered by some banks and lending institutions. This type of policy pays the balance of your mortgage to the lender if a person listed on the policy passes away.

Another option is term life insurance. With this type of policy you designate a beneficiary who is paid the value of the policy should you pass away. Some people prefer the flexibility to decide what to do with the insurance proceeds — the option of either paying off the mortgage or making the monthly mortgage payments and investing the money, for example. If the home has a low interest rate, the beneficiary may not want to pay off the mortgage; instead, he or she may want to sell the home or make other decisions with the insurance proceeds.

Mortgage life insurance covers you for the balance of the mortgage, which usually declines over time. Term life insurance provides coverage for the amount of the policy for a specific term, and not on a declining balance. Compare the cost differences, as well as the features.

Speak with an experienced insurance professional trained to review the options that are available and suitable to your individual and family needs. Ask questions and make sure you understand all the terms and conditions contained in your policy. Consult your lawyer should you want any advice or clarification of the legal contents of any policy.

13

Moving forward

Purchasing and owning a first home is a dream come true for many Canadians and it can be for you as well. Congratulations! You bought and read this book. That is a big first step.

This book was written as an objective-oriented, systematic guide. The chapters of the book were arranged in an action-oriented order. I have tried to provide you with specific action steps, information, and strategies to help you start your home-buying journey. Your next step is to put your plan into action.

If you go to www.RealEstateBuyerClub.com you will find updates, important home buying and selling information, calculators, and other helpful tips — all geared to help guide you through a pleasant (and hopefully stress-free) buying experience.

Are you ready to put together your buyer's team? Do you plan to find a real estate professional to assist you? If you wish, you can contact me for assistance with your first-time buying process through www.RealEstateBuyerClub.com.

You are not alone. I have access to a national network of experienced real estate professionals throughout the country who are available and willing to assist you with your home-buying plan. You will need to decide whether or not you want a real estate profession-al to *represent* you in the buying process. A buyer's agent will provide you with important market and real estate information, as well as guide you through the home-buying and closing process.

Again, you will also want to get *pre-approved* for a mortgage — either with a bank or through a mortgage professional. This will pro-vide you with the peace of mind that you are purchasing a property that you can afford. Remember to get the mortgage interest rate guaran-teed for a period of time (ideally 120 days), and the pre-approval should be in writing. Be sure to negotiate the important prepayment privileges and other mortgage options into your mortgage.

A lawyer is another important professional for your home-buying team; you may want to meet with a lawyer to establish a relationship in advance. Laws can and do change. Provincial rules, processes, and laws vary so having a real estate lawyer will help you keep current with these ever-changing rules and laws.

Collectively, your team of professionals will work together to assist and guide you through this important and exciting home-buying process.

I am always delighted to hear from and meet first-time home buy-ers. Feel free to email me any questions, comments, or suggestions. I also appreciate hearing your comments about the book so that fu-ture editions of *Your First Home: A Buyer's Kit* can be more informa-tive. Check the website frequently; perhaps register for an upcoming seminar or sign up to receive the First-Time Buyer's Newsletter at www.RealEstateBuyerClub.com.

It's up to you! You can do it! Real estate is a long-term investment. We have to live somewhere, so build your own net worth and life-style. Be optimistic and be positive! Create your Home Buyer Plan. Start today! Good luck and congratulations!

You can contact me at: Kimberley Marr, Broker
RE/MAX Professionals Inc., Brokerage
Phone: (905) 270-8840
Email: kim@kimberleymarr.com

Note: www.RealEstateBuyerClub.com is owned and managed by Kimberley Marr.

OTHER TITLES OF INTEREST FROM
Self-Counsel Press

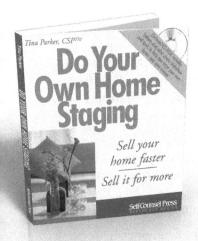

Do Your Own Home Staging

Tina Parker

ISBN: 978-1-55180-838-3

$24.95 CAD

Selling a home is harder than ever before, especially in today's real estate market. *Do Your Own Home Staging* demonstrates, step-by-step, exactly what you can do to sell your home faster and for a better price.

Just as you would dress yourself up for a job interview or a date, your home needs to be presented in the best possible way when you are trying to make the sale and get a great price. The tried, tested and mostly inexpensive techniques detailed in this book will help you:

- Show off your home's best features

- Downplay features that may be unattractive to potential buyers

- Make your home appeal to a wider range of people

Whether you are working with a real estate agent, or selling a home yourself, the home staging techniques described in this book will help you ensure that you get the best price. Included are checklists for each area of your home, so you can be sure that you've covered all the bases before putting your house on the market.

The CD-ROM included with the book includes before-and-after photos, checklists, and even more tools to help you as you go.